INDIA

INDIA

ITS HISTORY, DARKNESS AND DAWN

W. ST. CLAIR-TISDALL

GYAN

Published by

GYAN

Gyan Publishing House
5, Ansari Road
Daryaganj, New Delhi-110002
Phone: 011-47034999, 9811692060
E-mail: books@gyanbooks.com

Distribution Network
gyanbooks.com
India, USA, Canada, UK, Australia

ISBN: 978-93-7097-001-4 (PB)

First Published, 1901

2nd Impression 2025

Printed at: Gyan Press, Delhi.

INDIA
Arthur W. ST. CLAIR-TISDALL

INDIA

ITS HISTORY, DARKNESS AND DAWN

INDIA

ITS HISTORY, DARKNESS AND DAWN

BY THE

REV. W. ST. CLAIR-TISDALL, M.A., C.M.S.

AUTHOR OF

"THE RELIGION OF THE CRESCENT" "THE CONVERSION OF ARMENIA"

"THE SOURCES OF ISLÂM" ETC. ETC.

Ἡ σκοτία παράγεται καὶ τὸ Φῶς τὸ ἀληθινὸν ἤδη φαίνει.

1 JOHN ii. 8.

LONDON

STUDENT VOLUNTEER MISSIONARY UNION

22 WARWICK LANE, E.C.

1901

"O God, who hast made of one blood all nations of men to dwell upon the face of Thy whole earth, and who didst send Thy blessed Son to preach peace to them that are afar off and to them that are nigh, grant that all the people of Hindū, Buddhist and Muḥammadan lands may feel after Thee and find Thee; and hasten, O Lord, the fulfilment of Thy promise to pour out Thy Spirit upon all flesh; through Jesus Christ our Lord. Amen."

PUBLISHERS' PREFACE

THIS little book is one of a series of Text-Books published by the Student Volunteer Missionary Union, and intended primarily for the use of Missionary Bands in our Universities and Colleges.

It is hoped, however, that it will prove useful to all students of Missions. The Executive of the Union were fortunate in securing as the writer one so well qualified for the work as Mr. St. Clair-Tisdall, and they desire to record their deep indebtedness to him for having so readily responded to their request.

A series of Outline Studies for use along with the Text-Book has been prepared by the Educational Secretary; in this pamphlet a selected bibliography will be found.

This book is sent out with the earnest hope that it will prove a valuable guide to all those who desire a fuller acquaintance with India as a Mission-Field, and an incentive to greater effort for the evangelisation of the Indian Empire.

22 WARWICK LANE, LONDON, E.C.,
July 1901.

CONTENTS

PART III

Christianity and Christian Missions in India

INTRODUCTION

THE century which has just ended has well been styled the century of Missions. In our own day and generation we have, as it were, seen with our own eyes the fulfilment in great measure of the prophetic vision of the Seer of Patmos, when he beheld the angel flying in the midst of heaven commissioned to preach the everlasting Gospel to every nation, and kindred, and tongue, and people.[1] The more we think of the immense amount of work that has been done—the number of languages into which the Word of God has been translated, the millions gathered out of Heathenism, the many who have been found faithful unto death and have won the martyr's crown, the doors once fast closed and now widely opened, the mountains of difficulties apparently insuperable which have been levelled with the plain to make ready in the desert a highway for our returning Lord,—the more reason have we to thank God and take courage for the future. In all history God's Hand is visible, but nothing in history is more striking than what by the weakest of instruments God has accomplished in the nineteenth century. Our mistakes have been overruled for good, our want of faith has been rebuked, our weakness has been made strong, and our extremity has often been God's opportunity. No period from the time of Constantine the Great's conversion to the present day has seen such a widespread proclamation of the Gospel as our own age has witnessed. It has even been said that the rapidity of the spread of Christianity during the last hundred years does not merely equal, but largely exceeds, that during the first three centuries of the Christian era.

[1] Rev. xiv. 6.

The great success which, through God's blessing, has attended the mission work of the Church during the nineteenth century, has been chiefly and most markedly among heathen or idolaters in different parts of the world. It is well known, of course, that large numbers of Muslims too, especially in India and more particularly in the Panjāb, have been gathered in, and multitudes of those who have not yet been baptized have heard the Gospel message in Egypt, Palestine and Persia. But it has well been said that the Church at large has never yet in any adequate degree realised her responsibility towards Muḥammadans. There can be no question that the rise of Islâm was wholly due to the almost universal corruption of Christianity in and before Muḥammad's time. Islâm was undoubtedly used as God's scourge upon a Church full of idolatry and steeped in unutterable wickedness, a Church whose zeal and faith had degenerated into bigotry and superstition, and in which the worship of a simple Jewish maiden had almost usurped that of her Divine Son. The salt had indeed lost its savour. Had the Church remained true to her Founder's teaching, and had Muḥammad in his early days of sincerity and earnestness heard the pure Gospel instead of the inane traditions which, as the Qur'ân shows clearly, were by professing Christians[1] taught to him, he might have become the Apostle of Arabia. We know how, instead of that, he became the founder of a false religious system which throughout a large portion of Asia and Africa still disputes with Christianity the sovereignty of the human heart. The Church is only indirectly responsible for the existence of heathendom, inasmuch as not the origin but only the continued existence of such faiths as Taoism, Hindūism, and Fetishism, and of such philosophies as Confucianism and Buddhism, is due to her unfaithfulness and want of zeal. But the very existence of Islâm, now the greatest rival of Christianity, and of all faiths the most serious obstacle to the progress of the Gospel, is due to the falsification of the faith once for all delivered unto the saints. Is it not, therefore, the paramount duty of the Christian Church to evangelise all Muḥammadan lands within the early years of the twentieth century, and to win back for Christ the Bible Lands of the East?

Although the work has been commenced among Muslims in many lands, and although a considerable measure of success

[1] *The Religion of the Crescent*, pp. 162–169.

has attended it, yet this has been the case in spite of the want of method with which it has been undertaken. After the carelessness of ages, when the Church at length began to awake to her responsibilities, she had to set to work to learn the forgotten art of evangelising non-Christian nations. It was natural that it should take time to learn this. But after a century of experience it should be possible for us to correct the blunders of the past, and from them ascertain the proper course to pursue in the future. In all Nature law rules and method is manifested throughout the whole *κόσμος*. It cannot, therefore, be unfitting for us to use reason and experience to teach us how best to equip ourselves for the work we have to do, and what are the best methods to adopt in order, by God's grace, to bring the Gospel to bear on the minds, hearts and consciences of the False Prophet's followers. There can be no question that want of method has too largely characterised our work in the past. Men and women have been sent out to the mission-field with perhaps a fair knowledge of certain limited periods of Church History, or even with an extensive acquaintance with Greek and Latin philosophy, but with no real knowledge of Muḥammadanism, Hindūism, or any other of the great religious systems with which they expect to be brought into conflict. A study of a single one of the languages which they will have to use is thought entirely needless until the labourers arrive in the field and are engaged in the struggle. Not infrequently also a missionary who has spent years in working among Hindūs, for example, is sent—through failure of health, perhaps—to preach the Gospel to the Muḥammadans of Palestine, or the Buddhists and Shintoists of Japan. His message, of course, is the same. He has to preach Christ crucified to all alike. But it is too often forgotten that special preparation is needed in order to present the Gospel in such a way as to enable people to understand it. The missionary to Muḥammadans should at least know what elements of truth their religion embodies, lest in his zeal without knowledge he should run full tilt against all that is good and true, as well as against all that is base and defiling, in Islâm. But, in spite of our want of method and of the use of "sanctified common sense," much has been already accomplished, because, whatever else has been neglected, the absolute necessity of a heart-consecration—"spiritual men for spiritual work"—has been insisted on, at least by some societies. A man or woman called and sent of God into the mission-field, however badly equipped in many respects he or she may be, *must* be used to extend the knowledge of Christ. Their work, being done in Christ, is certainly not doomed to failure. Yet on the other hand, to use a blunt axe for want of a grindstone, or to work with a chisel when a saw is the proper instrument, can hardly be considered as the wisest possible course to pursue, though it is far better than sitting idle. Much has undoubtedly been done in the way of preparing for a victorious campaign against Islâm, for example. A good base of operations has been secured. It remains for us now to act wisely and energetically from that base, to make the best possible use of our troops, who, though few, must be efficient and properly trained and equipped, and so in the name of the Captain of our Salvation, advance to the assault and carry the Crusade to a successful end.

When Native Churches are formed, we should endeavour to render them really indigenous and independent, not merely feeble imitations of English congregations, bound to use, *e.g.*, a translation of a Prayer-Book which, however well adapted to English requirements, does not necessarily embody the very best possible form of worship for all men in all lands and under all circumstances. Some system of self-support also should be not only aimed at but attained. Learning wisdom from our errors in the past, we should avoid the fatal blunder of paying certain picked men, with foreign money, to preach the Gospel to their fellow-countrymen. We must teach every convert that Christ Himself has called and chosen him to be His witness, and has bidden him let his light shine forth before men. It may perhaps be necessary, at least at first, for foreign missionaries to find and pay teachers for schools, etc., but *never* for evangelistic work. This lesson we seem to have learnt in Uganda: in India we see only too clearly the evils produced by the contrary practice. When the Native Church has life (and a *dead* Church should be decently interred and got rid of as soon as possible), it will doubtless not only support its own pastors, but also send forth its own chosen representatives to preach the Gospel all around. Till then the missionary must do that work himself, with the aid of voluntary unpaid effort on the part of the converts. This has been done in at least one part of Africa, why should it not be done in Asia also? Till it is, the object at which we are aiming will never be accomplished.

In all our work—among Muslims especially—we should, at whatever cost, reject all connection with or countenance given to all that is false, unscriptural, and idolatrous in religious matters. Islâm, as we have seen, arose as a protest against a sacerdotal and semi-pagan Christianity. Even to the present day in Palestine Muslims are, I am informed on good authority, rather encouraged than otherwise to go to view the mummery and (as they themselves truly say) the idolatry which disgraces the Greek and Latin Churches in that land. But the object of letting the "True Believers" witness such things is that the sad and degrading sight may effectually deter them from any inclination they may have to embrace Christianity. That result is often attained. We know the use which the Spartans are said to have made of the spectacle of their unfortunate Helots' drunkenness in order to produce in the minds of their own sons a salutary horror of that loathsome vice. Such is the use which pious Muslims to-day make of the debased worship of the various Eastern Churches. We Protestant missionaries, therefore, especially in all Muḥammadan lands, cannot be too careful to avoid allowing ourselves to be in any way identified in the people's minds with those modern Helots in their superstitious practices, though always ready to afford to the members of these corrupt Churches any help in our power when they desire to adopt a purer worship. The Native Churches which God has called us to form must at all costs be kept pure and scriptural in doctrine and ritual. The warning may not be entirely uncalled for at the present day.

In order to found such Churches, we must preach the Gospel far and wide throughout Muḥammadan lands. For this we need men and women carefully trained, not only in the various languages used in those countries, but also in the Muḥammadan controversy. The Student Volunteer Movement should largely aid us in obtaining the workers we need; but when we have got them we should train them far more systematically than we do. There are plenty of retired missionaries of age and experience whose services might readily be enlisted for such a purpose. Missionary preachers and teachers should be quite as carefully and regularly instructed with regard to the religious ideas of the people among whom they are to labour as medical missionaries are trained in medicine and surgery. The latter are not sent out to begin their medical studies in the field, and to learn their profession by experimenting upon the *corpus vile* of the people among whom they are called upon to work. But this is just what is done with regard to all other missionaries. As we have already said, a man is sent to preach the Gospel to the Muslims, for example, who has never devoted anything worthy of the name of study to the great religious system of the people, and who does not know one word of any of their languages. Two years, often amid unhealthy surroundings and in a bad climate, are—at least in theory—spent in learning to speak the chief language in use in a missionary's particular part of the field, and during this time he is drawing full allowances from the society in connection with which he is to labour. Even then no system is adopted to ensure his mastering in any really satisfactory manner the chief tenets of Islâm, and no one has the right to insist on his learning them or even to volunteer to assist him in so doing. Nor would most overworked missionaries have time to do so. All this—or at least a good deal of it—should be and could easily be done before the would-be missionary enters the country at all. The Indian Civil Service candidate has to study a language or two before he leaves home for his post of duty, for even a wealthy Government would not incur the risk and expense of sending out untrained workers. But—on the ground of economy, too!—missionary societies do this very thing. When we understand our work better we shall doubtless adopt a different system, a more rational method, in this as in other matters.

One more most important method of spreading a knowledge of Christ among Muslims remains to be noticed—the utilisation of the power of the Press. Missionary societies have at last learnt the value of medical missions, just as they long ago learnt that of educational ones. But although we are all aware what invaluable aid the printed page gives to all Gospel work in Europe, we are only just beginning to realise how vastly important it is to provide a good vernacular Christian literature in the mission-field. It is not enough to appoint an aged and venerable missionary, too feeble for any other work, and who perhaps has never shown any particular literary aptitude, to translate a Commentary or two into the language of the country. We want something far more than that, something as sympathetic as in medical mission work. It is difficult to exaggerate the importance of the preparation of Christian literature of all kinds in such copious, expressive and polished languages as, for example, the Arabic, the Persian, the Turkish and the Urdū. Much has been done in the first and the last of these, but even in these two languages much, very much, still remains to be done. Nor is it enough to prepare such works and leave to chance the question of their publication and circulation. All these matters must be properly taken in hand and perseveringly carried out, if we are really in earnest in our resolve to win the Muḥammadan world for Christ.

Why should not some organisation or organisations be definitely set on foot in order to accomplish what is the great task—or at least one of the great tasks—which devolves upon the Church of Christ in this Twentieth Century, the conversion of the followers of Muḥammad? Only in this way can the work be effectually and systematically performed, only thus can the various important problems that present themselves be satisfactorily solved, only thus can an adequate supply of properly trained workers be obtained and maintained. The great measure of success that has already attended the establishment of the Medical Mission Auxiliary of the C.M.S. shows clearly what we need if the work of converting the Islâmic world is to be brought to a successful termination, and the disgrace to the Church of Christ, which the very existence of such a debasing parody of revealed religion constitutes, is to be erased from the pages of the future history of the human race.

It remains only to add a few words regarding the limits within which our space has compelled us to confine ourselves in this little book in treating of the vast subject of India. It has not seemed necessary to deal with the geography, climate, productions, commerce, and government of India, for the simple reason that so many other easily procurable manuals treat of these subjects much more fully than could be done here within the limits of a few pages. The student will find all that he will probably care to know with regard to these matters in Sir W. W. Hunter's able article on India in the twelfth volume of the *Encyclopaedia Britannica.* The subject of the languages of India is too vast in extent to be dealt with at all adequately here, but Appendix I. gives a few facts regarding them, and refers the student to the best general sketch of the subject. We have dealt with the three main religions of the country as fully as our space would allow.[1] The other religions are Sikhism, Jainism, Pārsiism, and Animism. Sikhism is professed by only about a million of people in the Panjāb itself; the few Jains in India are scattered in various parts of the country; the Pārsis, to the number of about 87,000, are found chiefly in Bombay; and Animism, a name given to the varying faiths of many of the aboriginal tribes, hardly deserves treatment in such a volume as the present. It would carry us far beyond our limits to deal adequately with these faiths, which after all are accepted by a comparatively small number of the population, and are dying out.

The bearing of the political history of India upon the social and religious condition of the people will be at once evident. Whether we wish to account for the variety of languages, of castes, of customs, of religions among the people, or to understand under what circumstances Christian missionary work began and has been carried on in India, we must know something of the history of the country. It will be seen how religion after religion, philosophy after philosophy, has been tried and has failed to elevate the people morally, or to satisfy either their intellects or their hearts. In studying the modern History of India, we notice how to one professedly Christian nation after another God has committed the task of preaching the Gospel, how each in turn proved unfaithful to its trust and lost its hold on the country; how our own East India Company opposed the spread of the Gospel, till in consequence the country was nearly lost in the Mutiny; and how differently things have turned out since the Gospel has been permitted to have free course in India. If we can in any degree see the finger of God in History, this should lead us to consider what our duty to the people of India is, and to strive to do it much more fully than has yet been done.

The use of diacritical marks over and under certain letters, in proper names for the most part, will not, it is hoped, perplex the student, while it enables us to use our own alphabet in such a way as to give a fairly accurate representation of the original spelling. In well-known names, as, *e.g.*, *Mysore*,

[1] Perhaps I may be permitted to refer the student for fuller information regarding Muḥammadanism to my *Religion of the Crescent* (S.P.C.K.), and on Buddhism to my forthcoming volume, the *Noble Eightfold Path*. The bibliography (Appendix II.) contains a large number of works on all such subjects.

Cawnpore, etc., we have retained the usual incorrect English spelling. The appended list will explain the pronunciation of the marked letters.

It is the Author's hope that this little book may be graciously used of God, and that it may, in some slight degree, help forward the Conversion of India to the Christian Faith.

W. St. C.-T.

Bedford, *July* 1901.

PRONUNCIATION

1. The Vowels are pronounced as in Italian, except that *a* short has the sound of *u* in *but*.
2. The *dotted* letters (*ṭ*, *ḍ*, *ṇ*) are *cerebrals*, pronounced by putting the point of the tongue to the palate.
3. *Dh*, *ḍh*, *th*, *ṭh*, *k'h* (and *gh* in *Indian* words) have the letters pronounced separately, as in "kille*d h*im," "in*k-h*orn," etc.
4. *Š̌* is a cerebral *sh*.
5. *C* and *Ch* are pronounced like *ch* in *church*.
6. *Gh* and *Q* in *Arabic*, *Persian* and *Turkish* words are deep gutturals.
7. An inverted comma (ʿ) in Arabic words represents the *ain*, a slight guttural sound which is not found in European tongues.
8. *Ḥ* occurs only in Arabic words, and is a guttural *h*.
9. *K̇h* is pronounced as *ch* in Scotch *loch*, German *Buch*.
10. *T̲*, with a stroke under it, is the thick Arabic *t̲*.
11. *Z̄*, *ẓ*, *ẓ*, *z̲* are different Arabic letters, but in India are all pronounced alike, as the English *z*.
12. *Ṛ* has a very slight *r* sound followed by *i*.

PART I

A BRIEF SKETCH OF THE POLITICAL HISTORY OF INDIA.

CHAPTER I

THE EARLY HISTORY OF INDIA.

OWING to the singular dearth of historical works among the vast mass of Sanskṛit literature, it is quite impossible to construct anything but a mere outline of the ancient history of India. The fact that there exist in India at the present day many tribes which speak languages different from those of the Âryan family, and that these tribes are mentioned in the early Sanskṛit poems as enemies of the Âryan invaders, proves that, long before the arrival of the latter, India had been peopled by non-Âryan nations. Of these the tribes of the Kōlarian stock must have arrived at a very remote period. They were followed by the Drāviḍians, who drove them to the forests and mountains. These seem to have been succeeded by the *Śakâ* (=Gk. Σάκαι, Lat. *Sacae*), an Indo-Scythian people, who overran a great part of the country. They are described as a white-skinned race, who were in some places absorbed by the succeeding Âryan wave of immigration, and became members of the *Kshatriya* or warrior-caste. Elsewhere, however, they long continued to contend against their Âryan foes. (In fact, though reputed to have been subdued by the great Vikramāditya, king of Ujjayinî, who died B.C. 58, they appear to have recovered their power soon afterwards, and to have been dominant in the North-West of India during part of the first century before and the first two centuries after the commencement of the Christian era. The Šakā gave their name to an era, which commenced A.D. 78, and was founded by their king Šāli-vāhana.[1] Gotamo Buddha's father, Suddhodano, belonged to this race.)

From the close connection which is evident between the language of the Ṛig-Veda, the oldest literary monument of India, and that of the Avestā, the sacred book of ancient Persia, it is probable that the Âryans did not invade India until after rather than before the year B.C. 1500. The common home of the whole Âryan race, or at least of the Indian and Īrānian branches thereof, was undoubtedly Herât and its neighbourhood, if we may accept the very early tradition on the subject contained in the Avestā. It is very probable that some far-reaching religious difference—possibly the reformation which is attributed to Zoroaster—was one of the main reasons why the Indian Âryans left their original home and invaded India. They entered the country through Afghānistān, and their earliest settlements were in the Panjāb. Thence they gradually spread over the whole country, subduing the earlier inhabitants, and in part destroying them in Hindūstān proper, though in the southern part of India their power was far less felt, as is manifest at once from the type of feature of its present inhabitants, and from their retention of their ancient, non-Âryan languages.

The two great Epic poems of Ancient India, the Mahābhārata and the Rāmāyaṇa, contain in a poetic and legendary form an account of certain great historical events; but to discover the exact character and date of these occurrences from the poems would be as difficult as to ascertain the precise historical basis which underlies the similar productions of Greece, Rome, and ancient Germany,—the *Iliad*, the *Aeneid*, and the *Nibelungenlied*. It has, however, been supposed that the historical[2] germ of the Mahābhārata consists of a conflict between two neighbouring tribes, the Kauravas and the Pañcâlas, in Northern India, which probably took place not later than the tenth century B.C. One of the leading personages in this Epic, Dhṛita-rāshtra, was brother of Pāṇḍu, father of the five Pāṇḍava princes, whose

[1] But the latter is called "King of the South" or Dakhan, and Vikramâditya is said to have been slain in battle against him. This shows how little reliance can be placed upon the legend.

[2] Macdonell's *History of Sanskrit Literature*, p. 285.

victorious contest with the Kauravas is detailed at length. Dhṛita-rāshṭra Vaicitravīrya is mentioned in the *Kāṭhaka* recension of the Black Yajurveda as a well-known person. (The oldest form of the poem may date from the 5th century B.C.[1]) The Rāmāyaṇa has been supposed to contain traces of a very ancient expedition of the Âryans through the South of India and as far as to Ceylon. But for many reasons this seems unlikely. Kings Ikshvāku, Dasaratha and Rāma, of Ayodhyā (Oudh), are mentioned[2] in the Ṛig-Veda, and are doubtless historical. (The kernel of the Rāmāyaṇa was probably composed[3] before B.C. 500.)

Darius Hystaspis of Persia (B.C. 521–486) is the first important invader of India known to us in historical times, for it is hardly possible to ascertain whether there is any foundation for the Indian conquests of the legendary Queen Semiramis mentioned by Ctesias and Diodorus. Elamite and Accadian princes may have carried their arms in the direction of Sindh, though we have no proof of the fact. But, whether or not we credit the account of the voyage of Scylax, Darius' admiral, on the Indus, there can be no doubt that some at least of the princes of the Panjāb and Sindh bowed to the yoke of the great Achaemenian conqueror. Darius is said to have carried his arms almost to the borders of Rājpūtāna, and he received a rich tribute from the subject provinces. In Herodotus' time the fame of the golden sands of the Indus had spread far and wide, and this formed a powerful inducement to the ambition of Alexander the Great, when he had conquered the Persian monarch of his time (Darius III. Codomanus; battle of Arbela, B.C. 331), to invade and subdue at least those parts of India which had submitted to the Persian sway. Advancing through Afghānistān into the Panjāb plain, Alexander reached the Indus near the present Atak in B.C. 326. Crossing the river and receiving the submission of Taxiles, whose kingdom extended as[4] far as the Jhīlam, Alexander advanced against Porus, sovereign of a kingdom which stretched to the neighbourhood of the present city of Delhi on the Jamna. A fierce

[1] *Op. cit.* p. 285. [2] *Op. cit.* p. 311. [3] *Op. cit.* p. 309.

[4] The people over whom Taxiles ruled were the Takkas, who are by some writers supposed to have been at least partly of Turanian or Scythian origin. Their capital Taxila (Takshāsila) was a large and wealthy city in the Rāwal Piṇḍī district, and the ruins of Deri Shāhān are supposed to mark its site.

struggle took place at the crossing of the Jhīlam,[1] resulting in the total rout of Porus' army and the capture of the monarch himself. Restoring the latter to his throne as a tributary, Alexander crossed the Chenāb and the Rāvī, defeated a Hindū force on the northern bank of the Biās, and advanced as far as the Satlaj. Here, however, his further progress was checked by the refusal of his Macedonian troops to follow him into the unknown regions of the East. The kingdom of Magadha, which he was preparing to invade, had been the native land of Buddha, and was then a powerful monarchy with its capital at Patnā, the Pāṭaliputra of Indian writers and afterwards known to the Western world as Palibothra. Turning back to the confluence of the Jhīlam and the Chenāb, Alexander embarked with a portion of his force and sailed down the Indus to the ocean.[2] The remainder of the army fought its way along the banks of the stream. Sending his fleet under Nearchus to the mouth of the Euphrates, Alexander himself marched through Bilochistān, and safely returned to Susa (B.C. 325). Though his conquests in India were not lasting, the Macedonian invader opened the country to the trade of the West. His success encouraged Seleucus I. to attempt to overthrow the Magadhan monarch Chandragupta[3] (Sandrocottus), who had extended his conquests over a great part of the Panjāb. But this attempt resulted only in an agreement to leave Chandragupta in peaceful possession of his territories in consideration of the payment of a yearly tribute of fifty elephants (B.C. 312). A marriage alliance between the two monarchs, and the residence of a Greek ambassador, Megasthenes, at the court of Chandragupta from B.C. 306 to 298, still further cemented friendly relations between them. To Megasthenes we owe almost all our knowledge of the India of that period. The coins and inscriptions of the Graeco-Bactrian kings, together with the frequent mention of the Yāvanas or Greeks in the Sanskṛit and Pālī writings, show how extensive was the influence which the

[1] About 14 miles west of Chiliānwālā, and 30 miles S.-W. of the city of Jhīlam.

[2] Alexander built a city called Bucephalia (after his famous charger Bucephalus) near the modern Jalālpūr, and another named Nicaea, now Mong. He also built Alexandria (now Uchch), near the confluence of the Five Rivers, and Patala, now known as Ḥaidarābād, Sindh.

[3] Chandragupta had overthrown the Nanda dynasty in Magadha in B.C. 316. He reigned till B.C. 296. But some authorities place the beginning of his reign in B.C. 321, others in B.C. 310.

Asiatic Greeks for many centuries continued to exert upon Hindūstān.

Chandragupta's successors, and especially Aśoka[1] the Great (B.C. 257–220), extended their sway over the greater part of India. After becoming a Buddhist, Aśoka spread that faith, in part at least by force, throughout his dominions; and the numerous Pālī or Magadhan inscriptions which he has left in various parts of the country attest the extent of his empire no less than his religious zeal.

On Aśoka's death his empire soon fell to pieces, and his dynasty ceased to exist about thirty years after his decease. The princes of the Sañga family, who ruled for about a century, were succeeded by another great dynasty, known as the Andhra line. Vikramāditya was the greatest monarch[2] of this dynasty, which lasted for a considerable time after the commencement of the Christian era.

Several of the Graeco-Bactrian monarchs (whose monarchy was founded about B.C. 256) invaded India, and for a time ruled over portions of the Panjāb. The most noted of these invaders were Demetrius, Eucratides, and Menander.[3] This empire gradually[4] gave place to that of the Parthian Arsacides, founded about B.C. 250 by Arsaces I. Nor were the Parthians also without their influence upon the Panjāb and Northern India; but our knowledge of their relations with India is too slight to enable us to give exact details of their invasions, and they established no lasting empire in the country.

During the whole of this period, and, in fact, up to the time of the English conquest, India was never subject to a single

[1] In his thirteenth edict, Aśoka mentions as his contemporaries Antiochus of Syria, Ptolemy Philadelphus of Egypt, Antigonus Gomatus of Macedon, Magas of Cyrene, and Alexander II. of Epirus. Antiochus Theos and Aśoka made a treaty with one another, apparently in B.C. 256.

[2] Either this monarch or one of his immediate successors may have sent the embassy to Augustus, mentioned by Strabo (B.C. 22–20).

[3] Eucratides, king of Bactria (B.C. 181–161), extended his conquests as far as Ḥaidarābād, Sindh, and is by some thought to have invaded Cutch and Gujarāt. Menander is probably the Milinda of the Pālī *Milinda-Pañho*, and it is thought he had his capital at Kābul. He may have reached Mattra in his incursions.

[4] The Graeco-Bactrian monarchy in Bactria itself fell before the assaults of a Tartar tribe called Sū about 126 B.C. About the same time they also suffered much in the Panjāb from the Tue-chi invaders. The Buddhist Council, held about A.D. 40, took place in the reign of a Tartar king named Kanishka.

ruler, but was subdivided up into numerous[1] kingdoms of varying dimensions, partly Âryan, partly Drāviḍian. But we have not data enough to enable us to obtain any very distinct idea of the limits of most of these states at any particular period, except perhaps with regard to the empire of Aśoka, which certainly embraced a very large portion of India.

After Aśoka's time India was for many centuries exposed to frequent invasions of the Huns or Tartars. The struggle between these invaders and the native population did not result in any permanent conquest, though the kingdom of Kanauj was overthrown by the former between A.D. 450 and 470. But the great battles of Korūr and Maushari between A.D. 524 and 544 freed India from these incursions. The country does not seem to have suffered much from foreign attacks between that period and the beginning of the Muḥammadan inroads, though we hear of a few attempts made by Persian monarchs, such as that which we now proceed to mention.

[1] Megasthenes speaks of 118 kingdoms in India in his own time.

CHAPTER II

THE MUḤAMMADAN PERIOD UNTIL THE ESTABLISHMENT OF THE MUGHUL DYNASTY. THE PORTUGUESE.

FROM about the beginning of the Christian era until the time of Chosroes I. (Khusrau Anūshīravān, A.D. 531–579) of Persia, our knowledge of the history of India is almost a blank, owing to the entire absence of history from the voluminous Sanskṛit literature. But during Chosroes' reign the Persians invaded the Rājpūt kingdom of Swāt. This invasion, however, does not seem to have had any lasting result. After a time the Persians retired, and peace was cemented by a marriage alliance between the Rājpūt prince Goha and one of Chosroes' grand-daughters.

When Yezdigird III., the last Persian monarch of the Sāsānian dynasty, was overthrown by the Arabs at the battle of Qādisiyyeh (A.D. 635), his empire fell into the hands of the Khalīfehs, the successors of Muḥammad. Not many years elapsed after this before the followers of the Prophet began that career of conquest which finally rendered them masters of almost the whole of India.

In the year A.D. 664 an Arab force advanced from Baṣrah into Sindh, but its only result was the plunder of a few towns. In 711, Muḥammad Qāsim led an army up the Indus as far as Alōr, then the capital of Sindh. The Rājā, Dahir by name, was slain in battle, and his capital and some other cities were taken by storm. Qāsim then invaded Gujarāt, and pressed on as far as Chitor. But his utter defeat there by the Rājpūts discouraged the invaders, and gave India a century's respite from attack. Again in A.D. 812 a battle was fought at Chitor between the Rājpūts and the Muḥammadans, who had invaded the country under the leadership of Maḥmūd, governor of Khurāsān. But the Indian forces again gained the day, and drove back the invaders. This was the last attempt made by the Arabs to conquer India.

A Turkish or Tartar slave, Alptagīn, founded for himself a kingdom in Afghānistān, with Ghaznī as its capital, about the year 961. His successor, Sabaktagīn, was suspected by Jaipāl, king of Lahore, of preparing for an attack upon the latter's territories. To avert this Jaipāl marched with a large army to Laghmān, between Kābul and Peshāwar. While the two armies faced one another, a sudden storm struck terror into the breasts of the Hindūs, and Jaipāl purchased peace by the surrender of his elephants and the promise to pay a considerable sum of money. When he returned home, however, Jaipāl refused to pay the money, and imprisoned the messengers sent to demand it. This led to a renewal of the war. Jaipāl's vast army was utterly routed at Laghmān, and the valley of Peshāwar was pillaged. For various reasons Sabaktagīn was unable to follow up his success, but his son and successor, the famous Maḥmūd of Ghaznī, defeated and captured Jaipāl almost at the same place in 1001. Set free on the promise of paying an annual tribute, Jaipāl soon after burnt himself alive, and was succeeded by his son Ânandpāl. The Rājā of Bhatnīr, chief of a Rājpūt tribe, refused to pay his share of the tribute, and thus involved himself in a contest with Maḥmūd, which, after a brave struggle on the part of the Rājpūts, ended in the conquest of their country. Maḥmūd, after subduing a revolt of the Governor of Multān, which city had been captured by him some time previously, then turned his arms against Ânandpāl, whom he accused of aiding his enemies. A great battle took place in the plain near the Khaibar Pass, and, after a terrible struggle, in which he lost 20,000 men, Ânandpāl was utterly routed. Maḥmūd plundered Nagarkōt and returned home in triumph. A few years later, in another expedition, he captured Thanēsar, and carried off an immense booty and 200,000 captives. In 1017 he once more invaded the country, and reached Mattra, plundering and laying waste the towns, and extorting tribute from Kanauj and other places which he did not capture. In 1021, Ânandpāl's capital, Lahore, fell, and the Rājā fled to Ajmīr. Gwālior surrendered in 1023; and in the great expedition of 1024 the Sulṭān plundered Somnāth. These invasions, however, were in the main predatory, for the Musalmān yoke was soon shaken off after Maḥmūd's death in 1030. Not long after that Delhi revolted; and Lahore, which was defended by a Muḥammadan garrison, was with difficulty held against the fierce attack made upon it by the allied Hindūs. Sabaktagīn's successors, expelled from Ghaznī by the rising power of a rival dynasty which had made Ghor its capital, established themselves at Lahore for a time; but in 1186 Shahabu'ddīn Muḥammad Ghorī, having conquered the Panjāb from Peshāwar to Multān, captured Lahore and carried off its ruler, Khusrau Malik, a prisoner to Ghor. Muḥammad then advanced across the Satlaj to attack the kingdoms of Delhi and Ajmīr. But, being defeated in a great battle at Narāyan, near Thanēsar, in 1191, he was obliged to flee beyond the Indus. In a second expedition in 1193, however, he defeated the allies on the scene of his former overthrow, and thereby laid the foundation of the Muḥammadan Empire in India. Pṛithirāj, king of Delhi, was put to death by the conqueror; Ajmīr was taken by storm, and Qutbu'ddīn, whom Muḥammad appointed to the command of his troops, advanced as far as the city now known as 'Alīgaṛh, and made Delhi the seat of his government. Returning from Afghānistān at the head of fresh troops in 1194, Muḥammad overthrew the ancient kingdom of Kanauj, and captured Banāras. The tide of conquest rolled on irresistibly to Gwālior, Chitor, Gujarāt and other places. Bengal offered but a feeble resistance to the arms of Qutbu'ddīn, who plundered Nadiyā, and fixed his capital at Gaur.

After the murder of Muḥammad Ghorī in 1205, Qutbu'ddīn was appointed sovereign of Hindūstān, and was crowned in 1206 at Lahore. Four years later, in 1210, he was succeeded by Altamish, who, during his reign of twenty-five years, conquered Mālwā and Gwālior, besides putting down a rebellion in Bengal. He also successfully defended himself against an Afghān invasion, and took Sindh from another Muḥammadan chieftain. He was very nearly incurring the enmity of Chingīz Khān, who, having conquered Khvārism and Afghānistān, drove Jalālu'ddīn, son of the ruler of those provinces, out of his patrimony. But Altamish refused to grant the exiled prince an asylum or to take up arms in his behalf, and thus suffered no injury from the resistless Tartar conqueror, except that the latter's troops made a hasty incursion into Sindh. Altamish died in 1236, and civil wars and dissensions among the rival claimants to the throne for about ten years gave the Hindū princes of Rājpūtāna and other dependent States the opportunity of rising in rebellion. They were, however, again subdued by a younger son of Altamish, Maḥmūd, who reigned for twenty years. His *wazīr*, Bālbān, usurped the throne on his master's death, and held it until his own death, twenty years later. A few years afterwards, in 1288, an Afghān chieftain, named Jalālu'ddīn Fīrūz, founded what is known as the Khiljī dynasty, which lasted until 1321.

In 1293, 'Alāu'ddīn, nephew of Fīrūz, began the conquest of the Dakhan (which had hitherto suffered little from Muḥammadan invasions) by the capture of the strong Marāṭhā fort of Deogaṛh, now Daulatābād. 'Alāu'ddīn murdered his uncle and his two cousins in 1295, and then succeeded to the throne, which he held for twenty years. Soon after his accession he conquered Gujarāt, but had then to defend his dominions against a great Mughul invasion, which was repelled in a fiercely contested battle near the Satlaj. Turning his arms against Chitor and plundering it, he was just on the point of marching to the support of a force he had sent to continue his conquests in the south, when, in 1303, another great Mughul raid recalled him to the north. This was repeated in 1305 and 1306; and on the latter occasion the invaders were defeated on the Indus with great slaughter. This left the monarch free to pursue the conquest of the Dakhan. His general, Kāfūr, subdued the kingdom of Warangūl, south of the Godāvarī, returning to Delhi with immense treasures. Next year he overran the Carnatic, and advanced as far south as Madura. Another expedition was undertaken in 1312 to complete the conquest of the Marāṭhās. In the same year 'Alāu'ddīn repressed with much bloodshed a revolt in the north. His severities for some years kept down all attempts at rebellion, but at last the Rājpūts and Marāṭhās shook off the Muḥammadan yoke in 1316, while the monarch lay on his deathbed. Kāfūr endeavoured to seize the sovereign power under pretence of acting as regent for the youngest son of 'Alāu'ddīn, but was murdered. Qutbu'ddīn, who then ascended the throne, put down the rebellion in Gujarāt and among the Marāṭhās. After a reign of four years he was murdered by Khusrau, one of his favourites, who was defeated and put to death in 1321 by Toghlāq, governor of the Panjāb, on the field of Indrapat.

The conqueror ascended the throne of Delhi under the name of Ghiyāṣu'ddīn. He was the founder of the Toghlāq dynasty. Having repelled a Mughul invasion, the new sovereign undertook the task of subduing the revolted provinces of Telingāna,

Bengal, Dakha and Jaunpūr. His son Jūna Khān failed to capture Warangūl in 1322, but succeeded the year following. The city was intrusted to a Muslim governor, and was given the name of Sulṯānpūr. The remaining provinces were subdued by the Sulṯān in person, but on his return he was killed at Toghlāqābad by the fall of a pavilion. His son Jūna Khān then ascended the throne (A.D. 1325) under the name of Muḥammad Toghlāq, and reigned twenty-six years. Muḥammad bribed the Mughuls to retire from the Panjāb, which they had attacked. He soon established his power over nearly the whole of Southern India. A great expedition to conquer Khurāsān was projected, but never undertaken. In 1337, Muḥammad lost nearly the whole army of 100,000 men which he had sent to conquer Chinese Turkistān. The severe exactions which these warlike measures rendered necessary reduced great numbers of his subjects to the direst poverty, and this was followed by several years of famine. Revolts broke out in Multān, Bengal, and the Dakhan, and also in Lahore, the Carnatic, Telingāna, and other places. Although these were most severely repressed, other provinces, one after another, rebelled, Mahārāstra and Gujarāt among the number. Muḥammad had hardly subdued these districts when Mālwā and the Dakhan expelled his garrisons, and Ḥasan Gangū established an independent kingdom in that part of the country, with its capital at Kulbarga. Muḥammad died[1] at Tatta, on the Indus, in 1351, having seen his empire falling to pieces. A Muḥammadan kingdom had arisen in Bengal, a Hindū monarchy in Bijayanagar, another in Telingāna, and other provinces were but awaiting an opportunity to renew their struggle for liberty. Fīrūz Shāh, Muḥammad's nephew, succeeding to the throne, was compelled to recognise the virtual independence of these states, though at least some of them continued to pay him tribute. His reign was fairly peaceful, though he ill-treated the Hindūs, whom his promises and threats failed to induce to become Muslims. His reservoirs and other irrigation works were of great benefit to Upper India. After a reign of thirty-six years, Fīrūz abdicated the throne in favour of his son Nāṣiru'ddīn in 1387. But in less than a year the latter was dethroned, and Fīrūz appointed his grandson Ghiyāṣu'ddīn to succeed him. Thereafter the country was torn with internal

[1] It was this monarch who made two fruitless attempts to remove the whole population of Delhi to Daulatābād.

strife, monarch quickly succeeding monarch, until Maḥmūd ascended the throne in 1394, and reigned for nineteen years. In his time independent kingdoms were established in Gujarāt, Mālwā, K'handēsh, and Jaunpūr.

It was in this reign that the famous Taimūr i Lang, or Tamerlane, invaded India. It is impossible adequately to describe the fearful bloodshed which accompanied his victorious progress. Delhi surrendered, and was for five days given over into the hands of the ruthless soldiery of the conqueror. Assuming the title of Emperor of India, Taimūr captured Mīraṭh and other places, and put their inhabitants to the sword. Having at length sated his thirst for blood and plunder, Taimūr withdrew from the country, leaving one vast scene of devastation behind him. Maḥmūd died in 1412, the last sovereign of the Toghlāq dynasty.

After more than a year of contest, a new dynasty succeeded in the person of Khizr Khān, a Sayyid, who had been left as governor of the Panjāb by Taimūr i Lang, and who professed to reign as the latter's viceroy. The Sayyid dynasty was overthrown in 1450 by Belōl Lodī, the Afghān governor of Multān, who founded a new royal line, the Lodī, under which Āgra became the capital of the monarchy. Belōl succeeded in subduing all the country between the Satlaj and the Ganges, as far as Benares, and he effected the conquest of Jaunpūr after an intermittent struggle of nearly twenty-six years' duration. His son Sikandar reigned for twenty-eight years, and was then succeeded by Ibrāhīm, during whose reign Bābar, one of Taimūr's descendants, having established himself as ruler of Kābul in 1504, invaded the Panjāb in 1519. Having made two other predatory expeditions across the Indus during the next five years, Bābar, in 1524, extended his depredations into Sirhind. He soon retired, however, leaving 'Alāu'ddīn as governor of his conquests in the Panjāb. When the latter attacked Delhi during the following year, he was defeated by Ibrāhīm. Learning this, Bābar returned in 1525 at the head of a small force of Mughul cavalry. He encountered Ibrāhīm's vast army at Pānipat, and utterly routed it, with the loss to the conquered of 16,000 men, thus putting an end to the Lodī dynasty and establishing that of the Mughuls, which (in name at least) continued to hold the sovereign power in India until 1857.

It was during the time when the Lodī dynasty ruled at

Delhi that the Portuguese first began to assert their power in the Indian Ocean. Doubling the Cape of Good Hope in 1497, Vasco da Gama reached Calicut in the May following; but it was not until the autumn of 1500 that Pedro Cabral succeeded in establishing a trading factory there, which, however, was soon stormed and destroyed by the Muslims. Cabral thereupon captured, plundered, and burnt ten Moorish vessels, and bombarded the city. After visiting Cochin and Kananōr, and there establishing commercial relations, Cabral returned home, leaving a few ships under Juan de Nueva to guard Portuguese interests at those two places. Juan succeeded in repelling an attack made upon him by the fleet of the Zamorin of Calicut, and in maintaining his position until a large Portuguese fleet, under Vasco da Gama, arrived in 1502. The latter destroyed a number of Muḥammadan ships, and bombarded Calicut in revenge for the insults offered by its ruler to the Portuguese flag. On Da Gama's departure, the Zamorin prepared to punish the Rājā of Cochin, his vassal, for having shown favour to the Portuguese. But the arrival of Albuquerque's fleet forced him to seek for peace. However, when the Portuguese commander withdrew, his enemy again assailed Cochin with a large number of vessels and an army sent him by the Rājā of Bijayanagar. The Portuguese, assisted by the timely arrival of another fleet from home, took part in defending their ally. They defeated the Zamorin, compelled him to retreat, and then bombarded Calicut and seized all the Zamorin's fleet (1503).

In 1507 the growing power of Portugal in India under the first Portuguese viceroy, Almeida, was in the greatest danger of extinction from an alliance against them formed by the Zamorin and the king of Gujarāt with the Sulṭān of Egypt and the Venetians, the commerce of all alike being most seriously injured by the Portuguese. The latter were defeated in a sea-fight near Chaul; but Almeida, after bombarding Dābal, routed the allies off the coast of Diu. Albuquerque, succeeding him as viceroy, took Goa from the Rājā of Bījāpūr and made it the capital of the Portuguese dominions in the East, which under him reached their greatest extent. They comprised a number of forts and factories along the western coast of the Indian Ocean, from Ormuz to Malacca. A Portuguese attack on Diu in 1521 was unsuccessful; and in the year 1522 the Rājā of Bījāpūr in turn failed to capture Goa. An attack by the Gujarātī fleet on Chaul in 1527 was also unsuccessful, while the Portuguese attempt to seize Diu in 1531 with a large fleet and a considerable army succeeded no better. An alliance with Bahādur Shāh, the sovereign of Gujarāt, however, soon enabled them to erect a factory at Diu. This was attacked in 1537 by a Turkish fleet; but Silveira, the Portuguese commander, bravely held out until relieved by the arrival of vessels sent to his assistance by the viceroy. Henceforth, for many years, the Portuguese held almost undisputed command of the sea, though they were often exposed to attacks on land. They contented themselves with acquiring only a small strip of land along the seacoast, never aiming at extensive territorial possessions, since their object in India was trade and not conquest.

The allied armies of Aḥmadnagar, Bījāpūr, and Calicut, in 1570, for ten months besieged Goa, but in vain. Attacks on Chaul and Chāle were not more successful, and their failure established the Portuguese ascendency, until, in 1604 the Dutch, and in 1612 and 1622 the English, defeating the Portuguese on both sea and land, ultimately overthrew their power in the East.

CHAPTER III

THE MUGHUL DYNASTY, UNTIL THE BATTLE OF PĀNIPAT (A.D. 1761).

THE Mughul Empire was founded by Bābar, the fifth in descent from Taimūr i Lang, when he overthrew Ibrāhīm Lodī at Pānipat in 1525, as has already been recorded. Delhi and Āgra soon opened their gates to the conqueror, who then proceeded very speedily to subject to his rule the provinces along the Ganges.

Beyond the Jamna, however, a great confederacy of the princes of Jaipūr, Marwār, and Mewār, under Rānā Sangā, the Rājpūt ruler of the latter kingdom, had been formed to resist him. Mahmūd, a chieftain of the Lodī family, joined his forces with those of Rānā Sangā, and the allies advanced to attack Delhi. A fiercely contested battle was fought at (Fathpūr) Sikrī, near Āgra, and ended in the defeat and rout of the Rājpūts. The Mughuls in 1527 stormed Chandērī, and then overran Oudh and Bihār. The Sulṭān of Bengāl was compelled to submit and surrender North Bihār to the conqueror. But Bābar's reign was of short duration, as he died in 1530, and was succeeded by his son Humāyūn.

Humāyūn gave the Panjāb and Kābul to his brother Kāmrān, Rohilk'hand to another brother, and Mewāt to a third. After succeeding in putting down rebellions in Bihār, Jaunpūr, and Bandalk'hand he overthrew Bahādur Shāh of Gujarāt at Mandisor, and captured the rock-fortress of Chāmpanēr. Recalled from his career of conquest by a rebellion, headed by an Afghān named Shīr Khān, who had seized Bengāl and Bihār, Humāyūn stormed Chunār on the Ganges and advanced to Gaur, then the capital of Bengal. But Shīr Khān surprised and cut to pieces the Mughul army at Bakshar (Baxar), and compelled Humāyūn to flee across the Ganges. Another defeat near Kanauj in the following year compelled Humāyūn to flee. He wandered from place to place, seeking a refuge and assistance to regain his throne, until at length he was hospitably received at Herāt by the Shāh of Persia, who gave him 14,000 Persian cavalry to enable him to renew the struggle (1545). Meanwhile his adversary had seated himself on the throne, under the title of Shīr Shāh, and had captured the Panjāb and overrun Rājpūtāna. At the capture of Kālinjar, however (1544), he was killed; his son Salīm Shāh reigned securely until his death in 1553, and was then succeeded by his brother Muḥammad Shāh, whose three years' reign was troubled by many successful rebellions in various provinces.

Humāyūn captured Kandahār in 1545 and Kābul in 1547. But fresh troubles and rebellions caused him to lose the latter city, which he did not regain till 1551. In 1554 he took Lahore, defeated Sikandar Shāh, nephew of Shīr Shāh, at Sirhind, and in July 1555 re-entered Delhi and regained his throne. He died in 1556, and was succeeded by his son Jalālu'ddīn Akbar, the greatest of the Mughul sovereigns of India.

Akbar was only fourteen years of age when he ascended the throne. His reign lasted from 1556 to 1605, and he was therefore the contemporary of Queen Elizabeth of England. The first seven years of his reign were spent in almost unceasing warfare with the partisans of Muḥammad Shāh and others of the enemies of his dynasty. The Hindū general of Muḥammad Shāh's forces, Hēmū by name, marched from Bengal to Āgra, captured Delhi, and pitched his camp on the field of Pānipat, so often the scene of contests upon which the fate of India has depended. Bahrām Khān, the Mughul general, there attacked the hostile force on the 5th of November 1556, and, although his own army was much inferior in numbers, gained a complete victory. Hēmū was captured and slain, and his army routed. Sikandar Shāh was soon driven from the Panjāb to Bengal, where he still maintained his independence for a while.

In 1560 Akbar asserted his right to rule alone, and Bahrām Khān, who had hitherto exercised the supreme power in his name, raised a revolt. This, however, was quickly suppressed. Akbar then subdued Ajmīr, Gwālior, Oudh and Jaunpūr. Mālwā fell in 1561. Putting down the revolts which not long afterwards took place in the latter two provinces, Akbar in 1568 stormed Chitor, compelling its Rānā, Udī Singh, to flee to the hills, where he soon after founded Udaipūr. Many Rājpūt princes now submitted to Akbar, who strengthened his position by encouraging intermarriage between the princes of his own house and the daughters of the Hindū rājās. Oudh and Gwālior fell into his hands in 1570; in 1572 he defeated the Sultān of Aḥmadābād and added Gujarāt to his dominions. But soon afterwards Mīrzā Ḥusain, Akbar's cousin, rose in revolt and laid siege to Aḥmadābād. Akbar's sudden attack routed the rebels. Peace thus secured towards the West, Akbar was enabled to turn his arms against the rebellious Paṭhān ruler of Bengāl and Bihār, Dāūd Khān, who was driven into Orissa. Akbar's able Hindū general, Todar Mall, captured Orissa in 1578. A mutiny among Akbar's own troops was put down, not without difficulty; and Mān Singh in 1592 completed the conquest of the Paṭhāns in Orissa.

Mīrzā Ḥākīm, one of Akbar's brothers, had meanwhile risen in revolt. He invaded the Panjāb in 1581, and for a time was successful. But Akbar in the same year drove him back to his stronghold, Kābul, which did not long hold out against the imperial forces. Akbar, however, on his brother's submission, made him governor of that city. Kashmīr was conquered in 1586, Sindh in 1592, and Kandahār was captured in 1594. Meanwhile Muẓaffar Shāh, the deposed king of Gujarāt, had risen in rebellion. He was not captured until 1593. Akbar's campaign in 1586 against the Yūsufzāī tribes was not crowned with success, for he lost a whole division of his army among the mountains of Swāt, and another was driven to take refuge in the fort of Atak. These turbulent mountaineers were at last held in check by a line of forts built to prevent their inroads.

Akbar now undertook the conquest of the Dakhan. His troops failed to capture Aḥmadnagar, but occupied Birār. In 1599 Akbar marched from the Panjāb at the head of an army, and sent a force to besiege Aḥmadnagar. The city was carried by storm, the district of K'handesh was conquered, and the whole of the Dakhan might then have been subdued, had not the revolt of Salīm, Akbar's eldest son, compelled the emperor to march against him. Peace was made; but not long afterwards Akbar died, in 1605.

Akbar was a great statesman as well as a victorious general. His disbelief in Muḥammadanism led him to establish something approaching to religious liberty throughout his empire. He permitted Christians and Brāhmaṇs to hold controversies with the *mullās*; and he even went so far as to endeavour to establish a universal religion, claiming some kind of worship for himself. He established a new era, in which the years were to be reckoned not from the *Hijra* but from the date of his own accession. The solar year was substituted for the lunar one. The laws inflicting penalties on all breaches of the Muḥammadan precepts enjoining fasting, pilgrimage, abstinence from wine and certain kinds of meat, were annulled. Circumcision was postponed until the son of Muḥammadan parents had reached the age of twelve years, instead of taking place on the eighth day from birth. Akbar also forbade the Hindū practice of compelling widows to burn themselves on their husbands' funeral piles, and he permitted widows to marry a second time. The poll tax (*jizya*) and all other taxes on those who refused to become Musalmāns were abolished. Hindūs were admitted both into the army and to take part in the civil administration of the State. Akbar's land revenue scheme was a great boon to his subjects, as were many other reforms which he introduced into the administration of justice. The army also was reformed, the soldiers well drilled, and their pay secured to them regularly. The system of canals which had been begun by Fīrūz Toglāq was developed and carried out extensively. The ruins of many magnificent buildings still bear witness to his taste in architecture. In a word, Akbar was the greatest and best ruler that India had ever had since the Muḥammadan conquests in that country began.

His son Salīm succeeded him under the title of Jahāngīr. Muḥammadanism again became the established religion of the empire. A rebellion on the part of his son Khusrau, a few months after Jahāngīr's accession, was put down with great cruelty. An attempt to subdue the Rānā of Udaipūr was unsuccessful; nor did the war with Malik Ambar, who ruled the Dakhan, at first succeed any better. At length, however, Jahāngīr's son Khurram compelled the Rānā to sue for peace. After some years of intermittent warfare, Malik Ambar was defeated, and compelled to purchase peace by the surrender of a large tract of territory. Jahāngīr's favourite wife Nūr-Jahān, whom he married in 1611, exercised an unbounded influence over him, mostly for good. But when Jahāngīr's severe illness in 1621 encouraged her to hope that his fourth son Shahriyār, the husband of her daughter, might be his successor, could his elder brother Khurram be removed, she began to endeavour to alienate his father's affection from the latter. A war followed, in which, after various changes of fortune, Khurram was obliged to surrender, and to give up his two sons as hostages. A little later Nūr-Jahān's ambition and jealousy of the military success of Muḥābat Khān, an Afghān general who had been employed against Khurram, led the latter, in revenge for an insult offered to his son-in-law, to rise in rebellion and seize the emperor's person. Nūr-Jahān, who voluntarily shared his captivity, soon managed to have her husband rescued. A fresh rebellion of Khurram, in which Muḥābat Khān took part, soon took place; but Jahāngīr's death in 1627 placed Khurram on the throne, under the title of Shāh Jahān. Nūr-Jahān died in 1646.

English intercourse with the Mughul Court began in Akbar's reign, when two Englishmen, Fitch and Newbery, visited Fatḥpūr about the year 1587. The East India Company, founded in 1600, sent out their first fleet of five vessels under the command of Captain Lancaster in 1601. Captain Hawkins was kindly received by Jahāngīr in 1609, and he received permission to open a factory at Surat. But Portuguese intrigues ultimately caused him to fail in his mission, and he left the country in 1611. Not long afterwards the Portuguese were defeated by Captain Best with a fleet of four vessels. This victory compelled Jahāngīr to entertain a greater respect for the English. Jahāngīr, by a treaty made in 1613, confirmed the English in the privileges which he had promised to Hawkins some years before. Surat then became the chief English factory in India. Near the end of 1615 Sir Thomas Roe, sent out by James I. as an envoy to the court of the Great Mughul, was granted an interview with Jahāngīr at Ajmīr. He remained for two years at the emperor's court, and obtained for the East India Company the right of carrying on trade throughout the country. Their first factory on the Eastern coast was founded at Armagāoñ near Vellore in 1625. In 1639 this was removed to Madras.

Shāh Jahān secured his accession to the throne by putting to death his brother Shahriyār and the sons of his deceased brother Dāniāl. A revolt headed by Khān Jahān Lodī ended in the defeat and death of the latter near Kālinjar. But 'Ādil Shāh of Bījāpūr, who had been favourable to the revolt, then rebelled, and was assisted by the Marāṭhā chieftain Shāhjī, who now ruled Aḥmadnagar. In 1636 'Ādil Shāh made peace with the emperor, and was rewarded by being given a part of the Aḥmadnagar State. Shāhjī submitted in the following year, and his dominions were annexed to the Mughul Empire. In 1632 the Mughul troops stormed the Portuguese factory at Hūghlī, near Calcutta, destroyed their fleet, and thus put an end to the Portuguese power in Northern India.

Kandahār was surrendered to the Mughuls in 1637, but in 1647 it was again taken by the Persians; nor could Shāh Jahān's utmost efforts succeed in recovering it. For two years he endeavoured without success to conquer Balkh. After this the emperor employed some years of peace in establishing in the Dakhan the revenue system which Akbar had introduced in Hindūstān proper. The Tāj Maḥall at Āgra, reared in memory of his favourite wife Mumtāz Maḥall, is the greatest monument of the art and architecture of his time.

Aurangzīb, one of Shāh Jahān's sons, was in 1653 appointed viceroy of the Dakhan. Then war soon broke out through a quarrel between Mīr Jumla, *wazīr* of the king of Golkonda, and his royal master. Aurangzīb took the part of the *wazīr*, captured and plundered Ḥaidarābād, and dictated harsh terms to the king. On the death of 'Ādil Shāh, Aurangzīb asserted that the emperor had the right to nominate his successor. To support this claim, Aurangzīb invaded Bījāpūr and laid siege to the capital. But the news of his father's serious illness compelled him to conclude a peace and hasten to Āgra, lest he should be forestalled in assuming the sovereignty by some one of his three brothers. The two elder, Dārā and Shujā', fought several battles with one another, till the latter, being defeated, retired to Bengal, of which province he was viceroy, in April 1658. Meanwhile Aurangzīb and his younger brother Murād, who ruled over Gujarāt, united together and defeated Dārā at Āgra in June of the same year. Aurangzīb then made himself master of Āgra, imprisoned his father and Murād, and in August was proclaimed emperor at Delhi. Shāh Jahān died eight years later.

Hardly was Aurangzīb seated on the throne when he had to march to encounter the army with which Shujā' was advancing from Bengal. A battle fought at Kajwa, near Ilāhābād (Allahabad), resulted in the total overthrow of Shujā', who fled to Arakan, and died there. Dārā's forces were defeated near Ajmīr, and that prince, betrayed soon afterwards into his brother's hands, was beheaded at Delhi. Murād was also slain, and Aurangzīb had now none of his family left whose claim to the throne might imperil his security.

But a more formidable adversary than any whom he had yet encountered appeared in the person of Šivajī, son of the Shāhjī already spoken of as having virtually become ruler of Aḥmadnagar in the reign of Shāh Jahān. From the fastness of Torna, near Pūna, where he had established himself with a band of Marāṭhā adherents, Šivajī continually encroached on the Bījāpūr territory, defeated a Mughul army under Afẓal Khān which had been sent against him, and in 1662 found himself at the head of an army of 7000 horse and 50,000 foot. He attacked Surat and plundered the native city, though the English and Dutch factories did not fall into his hands. His fleet plundered the Mughul vessels and pillaged Barsalor. His raids provoked the emperor to send a large force against him, and Šivajī surrendered many of the forts he had captured, on condition of obtaining a royal grant of the remainder and the recognition of his right to a fourth part of the revenues of Bījāpūr. Year by year the Marāṭhā warrior's power increased. He overran K'handesh, plundered Surat once more, and defeated a Mughul army of 20,000 men sent against him by the emperor. A Hindū rebellion in Rājpūtāna, caused in part by the reimposition of the *jizya* tax and by various other tyrannical acts on the emperor's part, involved the Mughuls in a long continued series of struggles with the Rānā of Udaipūr. The war with the Yūsufzāīs, which was not concluded till 1675, also divided the Mughul forces, and gave Šivaji an opportunity of gradually extending his dominions. He invaded Bījāpūr, subdued the Southern Kankan, and was solemnly crowned as Rājā at Rāipūr in June 1674. He overran Birār, K'handesh, and Gujarāt, allied himself with the Rājā of Golkonda, seized Vellore, Mysore, and the Carnatic, and compelled the Mughuls to raise the siege of Bījāpūr. He was then recognised as sovereign of all the dominions in the Bījāpūr territory over which his father had ruled. His death in 1680 freed Aurangzīb from the most formidable of his enemies.

Sambajī, who succeeded his father on the throne, was a sensual and cruel tyrant. But he almost destroyed a Mughul army under Mu'aẓẓam; and in 1682 he plundered and burnt Burhānpūr, and swept like a scourge through K'handesh, in defiance of the army which Aurangzīb was leading in person against him. Baroch was destroyed in 1683; but then the tide of fortune turned against the Marāṭhās. Aurangzīb carried Bījāpūr by storm in October 1686, conquered Golkonda in the following year, and in 1688 his conquests had reached as far as to Tanjore. Soon afterwards he surprised and captured Sambajī, whose eyes he put out, cut out his tongue, and then beheaded him. But the Marāṭhās were as far from being subdued as ever. Their light horsemen, harassing the advance of the Mughul armies, levied contributions throughout the whole of the Dakhan, and never gave their enemies a chance of meeting them in a pitched battle. Rājā Rām, Sambajī's brother, from Rāigaṛh at first, and, after its capture by the Mughuls, from Jinji in the Carnatic, directed the movements of his followers. When Jinji fell in 1698, Rājā Rām, from his stronghold of Satāra, continued his plundering expeditions until his death in 1700. His widow Tārā Bāi and his infant son Šivajī still continued the struggle; and when Aurangzīb withdrew to die at Aḥmadnagar in 1707, he did so with the sad consciousness of having failed to subdue his enemies in the Dakhan. His bigotry and intolerance had roused the fierce hatred of his Hindū subjects and overturned Akbar's wise and generous policy, and when he died his empire had begun that downward course of disruption and decay which none of his successors was wise and strong enough to check.

The East India Company was largely helped in its steady acquisition of power in India by the almost constant warfare which prevailed during Aurangzīb's reign. In 1661 the charter granted them by Charles II. empowered them to make peace and war in India, to administer justice in their possessions there, and to drive out all who tried to infringe their trading monopoly. In 1668 the king made over to the Company the island of Bombay, which had formed part of the dowry of his wife, Catherine of Braganza. They were permitted to coin money at Bombay in 1676, which city became in 1685 their capital in Western India. Its governor was appointed Governor-General of India in the following year. The same year saw an English fleet sailing up to Chittagong on the Hūghlī. A quarrel with the natives resulted in the bombardment of the town of Hūghlī. Bālāsor was bombarded not long afterwards, and the English had to retire to Madras. In revenge for the capture of some ships carrying pilgrims to Mecca, the Mughuls took the factory at Surat and nearly captured Bombay itself. In 1695 the villages which stood on the site of Calcutta were acquired by purchase, and the city was founded in 1696. During a rebellion in Orissa soon afterwards, the governor of Bengal accorded to the English permission to fortify Calcutta, or Fort William as it was then called. Bengal was created a Presidency in 1681, and Calcutta became its capital in 1705. Madras had been founded as early as 1639. The French, who were at first friendly rivals of the English, founded Pondicherri in 1672.

Aurangzīb had in his will divided his empire into three parts. His eldest son, Mu'aẕẕim, was declared emperor, and Delhi was assigned him as his capital. Bījāpūr and Golkonda were given to Kāmbakhsh, while 'Āẕim was to reign at Āgra over the southern portion of the empire. 'Āẕim, however, claiming to succeed his father as ruler of the whole country, was defeated and slain in battle by Mu'aẕẕim near Āgra. A battle near Ḥaidarābād was fought between the conqueror and his third brother, and ended in the latter's defeat and death. Mu'aẕẕam then became sovereign of the whole of the Mughul dominions, and assumed the title of Bahādur Shāh.

The new emperor set up Sāho, one of Sambajī's sons, as Rājā of Satāra, thus dividing the Marāṭhās, and delivering himself from all fear of their attacks. He subdued the rebellious chiefs of Jaipūr and Mārwār, and then marched against the Sikhs, who had attacked Sirhind. The latter people, disciples of Gurū Nānak, having been persecuted by the Muslims, had turned under Gurū Govind into a nation of warriors, the deadly foes of their persecutors. Defeated by Aurangzib, they had now embraced the chance afforded them by the dissensions among his sons, and were pillaging the country and destroying mosques. Bahādur Shāh defeated them, captured their chief mountain stronghold, and compelled them to remain quiet for a time. His death in 1712 gave rise to fresh civil strife, for his sons contested with one another the possession of the throne. The eldest, Jahāndār Shāh, defeated and slew his brothers, but was himself killed six months later by his nephew Farrūkhsīr.

The new emperor owed his elevation to the throne to the aid of two Sayyid brothers, Ḥusain 'Alī Khān and 'Abdu'llāh Khān. Ḥusain was sent to subdue the Rājā of Mārwār, and the latter submitted on receiving favourable terms. Ḥusain was then made viceroy of the Dakhan, where he concluded a peace with Sāho, and acknowledged Sambajī as Rājā of

Kōlāpūr. The Sikhs under Bandū made another incursion into the lowlands, but were defeated; their leader was captured and put to death. During the whole of this time, the emperor had been secretly plotting the destruction of both Ḥusain and 'Abdu'llāh, the latter of whom was his prime minister. But these schemes were discovered; Farrūkhsīr was cast into prison by Ḥusain, and soon after put to death. Two of his successors died within a few months, and then Muḥammad Shāh ascended the throne. It would be wearisome to relate in detail the plots and counterplots which now set in, and the struggles which were carried on by the various petty chiefs in different parts of the country, each striving for independence. Qilīj Khān, governor of the Dakhan, and afterwards of Mālwā with the title of Niẓāmu'l Mulk, became the head of a virtually independent monarchy, with its capital at Ḥaidarābād. The dynasty which he founded there in 1712 still continues to exist. Sa'ādat 'Alī Khān, Nawâb of Oudh, made himself independent in 1720. Still earlier Ajīt Singh of Mārwār had established his throne at Ajmīr. Bājī Rāo, Pēshwā of the Marāṭhās, succeeding to that office in 1720, had ravaged Mālwā and rendered Gujarāt tributary. Pilājī Gaikwār became the founder of the dynasty which still rules at Baroda, Rāo Holkar of that at Indore, and Rānājī Sindhia established his dynasty at Gwālior. Bengal also became virtually independent under the Nawâb 'Alīverdī Khān, whose capital was Murshīdābād, and who also ruled over Bihār and Orissa. Thus began the dismemberment of the Mughul Empire.

Encouraged by the weakness of Muḥammad Shāh, the great Persian monarch Nādir Shāh, having conquered Afghānistān, crossed the Indus and defeated the Mughul army at Karnāl. Delhi was plundered, and tens of thousands of its inhabitants were put to the sword (1739). Nādir then retired, carrying with him an immense booty, and attaching to his own empire Sindh, Kābul, and the Panjāb as far as the Indus.

Muḥammad Shāh died in April 1748, and was succeeded by his son Aḥmad, who was deposed and blinded by his *wazīr*, Ghāzīu'ddīn. The latter then made one of Jahāndār's sons emperor, with the title of 'Ālamgīr. He is generally known as 'Ālamgīr II., the first of the name being Aurangzīb.

While the power of the Mughuls was declining, that of the Marāṭhās had so increased that they were now the dominant nation in India. The Brāhmaṇ Peshwās had long ruled in the name of Rājā Sāho, who was but a *roi fainéant*. When his death took place in 1749, and his grandson Rājā Rām II. mounted the throne at Satāra, the Peshwā, Bālājī Rāo, still continued to exercise sovereign authority, Pūna being the seat of his government and the real capital of the Marāṭhā dominions. Bālājī aided the English in capturing Savandrūg in 1755, which had been the stronghold of the pirate chief Angria. About the same time the English under Admiral Watson and Colonel Clive—afterwards so distinguished in India for his martial exploits—took Giriyah from the pirates and handed it over to the Peshwā, as it had formerly belonged to the Marāṭhās. A short time previously the Peshwā's brother, Rāghunāth Rāo, had taken Aḥmadābād from the Mughuls, and had compelled the Hindūs of Bhartpūr and Rājpūtāna to pay tribute.

Meanwhile the ruler of Afghānistān, the Dūrānī chief Aḥmad Shāh, in revenge for an attack upon his territories in the Panjāb, had plundered Delhi and appointed a Rohilla chief, Najību'ddaulah, as his governor there. Ghāzīu'ddīn the wazīr, who ruled in the puppet emperor's name, then called in the aid of the Marāṭhās. Rāghunāth Rāo expelled the Afghāns from Delhi, advanced into the Panjāb, took Lahore, and sent an expedition into Rohilk'hand (1751). Sedāsheo Bhāo, another Marāṭhā chieftain, captured Aḥmadnagar and a large part of the Mughul dominions in the Dakhan (1760).

But the Nawâb of Oudh, Shujā'u'ddaulah, expelled the Marāṭhās from Rohilk'hand. Ghāzīu'ddīn murdered the Emperor 'Ālamgīr, and Aḥmad Shāh advanced to Delhi and once more captured that city. But it was soon recovered by Sedāsheo Bhāo, aided by the Rājpūts and Jats. The Marāṭhā leader proclaimed Bālājī's son, Vishvās Rāo, emperor, and advanced with his whole army to meet Aḥmad Shāh in the field of battle. After two months' delay, during which time the two armies lay facing one another on the historic field of Pānipat, the struggle between the Hindūs and the Muḥammadans took place on the 6th of January 1761. After a fierce struggle in which both Sedāsheo Bhāo and Vishvās Rāo fell, the Marāṭhā army was utterly routed with terrible loss. This defeat broke for a time the power of the Marāṭhās, though it did not restore that of the Mughuls.

These continuous wars had so weakened the native States and divided them from one another that they could not offer any adequate resistance to the rising power of England and

France, which nations were rivalling one another in the extension and consolidation of their recently acquired dominions in India. We must now consider the parts that the English and French Companies respectively played in the contest which resulted in the foundation of the English Empire in India. From the time when the battle of Pānipat, just mentioned, was fought, the interest of the narrative is transferred from the declining Mughul and Marāṭhā kingdoms and their internecine struggles to the contest that long continued between the two nations which then represented Europe in the East.

CHAPTER IV

WARS BETWEEN THE ENGLISH AND FRENCH IN INDIA.

When war broke out between England and France in Europe in 1745, Labourdonnais, the French governor of Mauritius, assembled a fleet and sailed to Pondicherri. With the support of Dupleix, the governor of this French settlement, he then attacked Madras (Sept. 1746), which was garrisoned by only a few hundred Englishmen under Governor Morse. Madras fell in a few days, and Labourdonnais, having quarrelled with Dupleix, withdrew. Dupleix had promised to surrender Madras to his ally Anwāru'ddīn, Nawâb of the Carnatic, but broke his agreement and routed a large army sent against him by the Nawâb. Another victory gained soon afterwards over the Nawâb's troops on the banks of the Adyar encouraged the French Governor-General to attack Fort St. David. The Nawâb advanced to its relief, and the French were compelled to retire. A second attempt made in March 1747 was defeated by the arrival of an English fleet from Calcutta.

Admiral Boscawen with a large fleet and a considerable land force laid siege to Pondicherri in 1748, but failed to capture the place. The peace of Aix-la-Chapelle restored Madras to the English in the same year.

But Dupleix was ambitious of founding a French Empire in India, and of expelling the English from the country. Civil dissensions in the neighbouring native States, in which the French and English took opposite sides, renewed the war between the two nations in India. The Rājā of Tanjore had been driven from the throne by a rival, and Major Lawrence, on the plea of wishing to restore him, took Devikatta, which Partāb Singh, the Rājā's brother and successor, confirmed in the possession of the English. When Qilīj Khān the Nizâmu'l Mulk died, Dupleix aided Muzaffar Jang to seat himself on the throne of the Dakhan with the title of Sūbahdār. Chanda Ṣāḥib, appointed governor of the Carnatic under the Sūbahdār, rewarded the French for their assistance by giving them a grant of 81 villages. But Nāṣir Jang, who aspired to the sovereignty of the Dakhan, making common cause with Muḥammad ʻAlī, one of the sons of Anwāru'ddīn (who had fallen in the struggle), called in the assistance of the English. The latter enlisted as their allies a body of Marāṭhā horse. A mutiny among the French troops enabled the party of Nāṣir Jang to gain a victory and to advance against Pondicherri. They were, however, repulsed; and soon after the French commander Bussy routed a large force led by Muḥammad ʻAlī, and captured the fortress of Jinjī. Nāṣir Jang advanced to regain the fort, but was defeated, and he was slain by one of his own traitor nobles. Dupleix then appointed Muẕaffar Jang to the vacant throne. French influence thus became paramount for a time in Southern India. Early in 1751, however, Muẕaffar Jang was slain near Aurangābād, his capital, and Ṣalābat Jang was raised to the throne by the French, in his uncle's place.

Just at that moment Muḥammad ʻAlī, who had engaged the English to support him in his claim to the Carnatic against Chanda Ṣāhib, was attacked in Trichinopoly by his rival, whose capital, Arcot, was meanwhile bravely seized by Captain Clive and a small English force. Clive fortified the city; and, after withstanding for fifty days the determined siege and fierce assaults of a large army under Rājā Ṣāḥib, son of Chanda Ṣāḥib, beat off the enemy. Aided by the Marāthās and receiving reinforcements from Madrās, Clive inflicted two severe defeats on Chanda Ṣāḥib and his French allies. Major Lawrence joined him with fresh troops, and the French, who were besieging Trichinopoly, were surrounded and compelled to surrender. Another attack upon Trichinopoly was thwarted by the English, and the struggle in the Carnatic continued with varying results for some years longer. At length in 1754 (August), Dupleix was superseded by a French envoy Godehen, who concluded a treaty with the English, acknowledging Muḥammad ʻAlī as Nawâb of the Carnatic. Both parties agreed to abstain for the future from sharing in the contests which might occur between various native rulers. Bussy had meanwhile maintained the French nominee Ṣalābat Jang on the throne of Aurangābād, and had been appointed by him governor of the Northern Sircārs.

War soon broke out afresh. The French supported the

Regent of Mysore in his claim to the possession of Trichinopoly in 1755, but the English upheld Muḥammad 'Alī in his refusal to surrender that city. In 1756 De Leyrit, the new governor of Pondicherri, prevented the English from gaining possession of Vellore. Another French attack on Trichinopoly also failed, but in 1757 the French succeeded in gaining most other places of importance in the Carnatic.

We must now turn to Bengal, where a struggle for existence had begun between the English and the Sūbahdār, Surāju'd-daulah. On Aurangzīb's death in 1707, Murshid Qulī Khān had made himself virtually independent as ruler of Bengal, with his capital at Murshidābād. 'Alī Verdī Khān usurped the government from Murshid's grandson in 1740. On the occasion of a Marāṭhā invasion, the English had obtained permission to defend Calcutta by digging what was afterwards known as the "Marāṭhā Ditch." Surāju'ddaulah, who succeeded his grandfather in 1756, commanded Drake, governor of Calcutta, to level with the ground certain additional defences he had raised around Calcutta. When this and other demands were not acceded to, Surāju'ddaulah advanced against Fort William at the head of an army of 50,000 men. Drake fled, and the fort was soon captured. The 146 prisoners were shut up in the famous Black Hole for the night, whence only 23 came out alive in the morning (22nd June 1756). Not until January 2nd of the next year did Colonel Clive and Admiral Watson regain possession of Calcutta for the English. On the 10th of the same month Captain Eyre Coote stormed Hūghli. Surāju'ddaulah's camp was attacked near Calcutta by Clive's forces on the 4th of February, and the Sūbahdār was compelled to retreat. A few days later he made a treaty with the English, granting them the right to coin money and to fortify Calcutta, besides promising them the payment of a large sum of money in reparation for the loss of their property.

This enabled the English to carry on war against the French settlements in Bengal. Chandanagor was attacked both by land and sea, and on the 23rd of March in the same year its French garrison surrendered after a gallant defence. Surāju'ddaulah had meanwhile been negotiating with Bussy, and therefore Clive intrigued with his rival, Mīr Ja'far, with the object of dethroning him and placing the latter on the throne in his stead. Learning that the Sūbahdār had assembled his army at Plassy (Palāsī), to the south of Murshidābād, and was preparing to attack the English, Clive resolved to anticipate him by himself striking the first blow. Advancing from Chandanagor with an English force of only 1000 men, and aided by some 2000 native troops, he, on the 23rd June 1757, encountered the Sūbahdār's army, which consisted of 50,000 foot, 18,000 horse, and 53 guns, and gained a complete victory with but slight loss. Surāju'ddaulah fled to Murshidābād, but was soon after slain. Clive then placed Mīr Ja'far on the throne[1] as ruler of Bengal, Bihār, and Orissa, and the English influence in those regions became supreme. Major Coote expelled the French from Bihâr. Colonel Forde was despatched to attack them in the Northern Sircārs. He took Masulipatam from them, and compelled the Nizâm to cede a large tract of the surrounding country to the Company (1758–59).

In 1759 Shāh 'Alām, son of the emperor of Delhi, invaded Bengal with the aid of the Nawâb of Oudh, and laid siege to Patnā. But on the news of Clive's advance he fled without striking a blow.

Mīr Ja'far had now begun to plot in order to shake off the Company's yoke. At his invitation the Dutch at Chinsūrah sent a fleet of seven men-of-war, laden with soldiers, up the Ganges to assist the Sūbahdār; while they also marched out of Chinsūrah against the English. But Clive captured every one of the vessels, and Colonel Forde inflicted two severe defeats upon their land forces. The Dutch governor of Chinsūrah was compelled to sue for peace, and from that time the Dutch existed in Bengal only on sufferance.

In the South the struggle between the English and the French was carried on with varied success, but it ultimately ended in the triumph of the former. Lally took Fort St. David and Denikatta, and laid siege to Tanjore, but was obliged to retire on the advance of an English force to its relief. Muḥammad 'Alī surrendered Arcot to the French, and Lally laid siege to Madras towards the end of 1758. The city was gallantly defended by Colonel Lawrence, and the arrival of an English fleet in February of the succeeding year saved the place

[1] A patent of investiture was granted by the Mughul emperor to Mīr Ja'far. The latter gave the Company the *zamīndārī* proprietorship of 24 Pargānas or districts (a tract of 882 square miles) around Calcutta, and assigned the superior lordship of the same territory to Clive himself in 1759. The latter had been (in 1758) appointed first Governor of the Company's possessions in Bengal.

at a critical moment. Eyre Coote captured Wandiwash, and routed a French army led by Bussy, who was captured but subsequently released. Karikal was taken by the English in April 1760, and the French capital, Pondicherri, surrendered on the 16th January 1761. This final blow put an end to the struggle by destroying the French power in India and leaving the English victorious. As we have seen, the defeat of the Marāṭhās at Pānipat in the same year had overthrown the only really dangerous foes the English had to dread, or had at least weakened them too much to permit them successfully to withstand the steady growth of the British dominions in India. Nor was the Mughul emperor, Shāh ʻĀlam, a very formidable foe. In January 1760 he had again besieged Patnā at the head of a large army, but had been completely routed by Captain Knox with a mere handful of men. English influence was supreme in Bengal and Bihār, where they had dethroned Mīr Jaʻfar in October 1760, and put his son-in-law, Mīr Qāsim, on the throne; the Carnatic under Muḥammad ʻAlī was under their protection; and the Māraṭhā States of Orissa, Pūna, Tanjore, Kolāpūr, Satāra, Gujarāt, Mālwā and Birār were unlikely to unite together to oppose the common foe. Ḥaidar ʻAlī had recently made himself ruler of Mysore, and might become dangerous; less was to be feared from Ṣalābat Jang of the Dakhan; nor did it seem that the Jāt State, with its capital at Bhartpūr, was likely to become hostile to the English. Such was the position of affairs in India at the time when the fall of the French power in that country removed from their path the only powerful European nation then in a position to oppose their ambitious projects in the East. The British Empire in India may be said to date from the Battle of Plassy in 1757, though it was not finally established without the fierce struggles which ended with the suppression of the Mutiny a century later.

CHAPTER V

FROM THE BATTLE OF PLASSY UNTIL THE SUPPRESSION OF THE MUTINY.

THE new Nawâb of Bengal, Mîr Qāsim, removed his seat of government from Murshidābād to Manghîr in 1761, and began to prepare to throw off the Company's yoke by drilling and arming his forces in the European manner. War broke out in July 1763.[1] Defeating the Nawâb's army at Katwa on the 19th of that month, and occupying Murshidābād, the English replaced Mîr Ja'far on the throne. On August 2nd they again defeated the Nawâb at Giriyah. In revenge for this the Nawâb massacred his English prisoners at Patnā in October 1763.[2] The agent intrusted with the accomplishment of the cruel deed was Walter Reinhardt, a native of Luxemburg, more commonly known as Sumru. Shortly before this, Major Adams had routed the Bengāl forces at Rājmaḥall. He took Patnā by storm on the 6th November of the same year, and compelled Mîr Qāsim to take refuge at the court of Shujā'u'ddaulah of Oudh.

In May 1764 Shujā'u'ddaulah advanced to the siege of Patnā, but failed to take that place. In August of that year Major Munro, having sternly[3] suppressed a mutiny among his troops, advanced to Bakshār (Baxār), where, on the 23rd, he defeated the Nawâb-wasîr's army of 50,000 men, strengthened as it was by a force of Afghān cavalry. Next

[1] The immediate cause of the war was the Nawâb's refusal to permit the Company's private servants to carry on inland trade without the payment of imposts and customs dues. His troops began the war by firing on an English vessel.

[2] About 2000 Sepoys were massacred at Patnā, and some 200 Englishmen in the province.

[3] He blew 24 of the ringleaders from the guns. This outbreak is known as the first Sepoy Mutiny.

year Shujā'u'ddaulah, having engaged Malhar Rāo of Gwālior to declare war against the English, and obtained a large force of Rohillas to assist him, again advanced to the attack. But the Marāṭhās were repulsed by Carnac, Shujā'u'ddaulah was repeatedly defeated, and finally Lord Clive, who returned from furlough in May as Governor and Commander-in-Chief in Bengal, concluded a treaty with him which was very favourable to the Company. In August the emperor, Shāh 'Ālam, in return for certain payments, made over to the Company the *dīwānī* or fiscal government of Bengal, Bihār, and Orissa, to the nominal sovereignty of which provinces they had appointed Najmu'ddaulah instead of his father, Mīr Ja'far, who had now died.

In 1766 Lord Clive, with the aid of his Sepoys, suppressed a mutiny among the officers under his command. He then reformed some of the most scandalous abuses which had crept in among the Company's servants in Bengal, putting down their practice of taking bribes and engaging in private trade. Early in 1767 he finally retired and returned to England. The sad story of his last days is too well known to need repetition here.

Meanwhile a serious danger had arisen in the South. Ṣalābat Jang had been dethroned in 1762 by his brother, Niẕām 'Alī, who murdered him in 1763. Niẕām 'Alī then made an incursion into the Carnatic, but had to retire before the English forces. The Northern Sircars had been made over to the Company in 1766 by Shāh 'Alam, but Niẕām 'Alī threatened war if the English took possession of what he claimed as part of his own territory. An agreement was finally made, in virtue of which the Company received those districts on the payment of an annual tribute, and they formed a defensive alliance with Niẕām 'Alī.

The latter also allied himself with Mādhu Rāo, Peshwā of Pūna, in order to check the increasing power of Ḥaidar 'Alī of Mysore. The Marāṭhās invaded Mysore at the beginning of 1767, and retired laden with spoil. The Niẕām of the Dakhan soon after united with Ḥaidar 'Alī against the English, and attacked them at Changāma, but was severely defeated on the 3rd September, and again at Trinomalli on the 26th of the same month. Ḥaidar 'Alī's attack on Ambūr in December was not more successful. The Madras Government then renewed their treaty with the Niẕām against Ḥaidar 'Alī (February

1768). But in April of the following year the latter's successes compelled the Madras Government to accept the terms of peace which he dictated to them, including the acknowledgment of his right to all the territory he had claimed, and the formation of a defensive alliance with him.

A terrible famine in Bengal in 1770 caused the death of about one-third of the native population. This and the growth of abuses in the government was the cause of the appointment of the famous Warren Hastings, in April 1772, to the position of President of the Calcutta Council. The Company's officers took over the government of Bengāl and Bihār, Calcutta became the recognised capital of the province, and the Nawāb was stripped of all power. Great reforms in the fiscal department and in that of the administration of justice were introduced. Less deserving of praise was the part which Hastings took in hiring a body of English troops to Shujā'u'ddaulah in order to enable the latter to conquer Rohilk'hand. Colonel Champion in command of this force defeated Ḥāfiẓ Raḥmat Khān, the Afghān chief who ruled Rohilk'hand, at Rāmpūr (23rd April 1774), and the district passed into Shujā'u'ddaulah's possession.

Meanwhile the Marāṭhās had again come to the fore in both Upper and Lower India. They had overrun Rājpūtāna and the Bhartpūr territory, and had invaded Rohilk'hand not long before. They had placed Shāh 'Alam on the throne of Delhi, where he was but their tool. They compelled him to cede to them the districts of Korah and Ilāhābād, but their attempt to take possession of those districts was prevented by the English. The Peshwā Mādhu Rāo himself, at the head of another army, had in 1771 invaded Mysore and compelled Ḥaidar 'Alī to submit to the loss of a large portion of his kingdom and the payment of a heavy tribute. The latter's appeal to the Madras Government for help was not acceded to, in spite of the treaty which entitled him to expect their assistance. This breach of faith rendered him ever afterwards the determined enemy of the English.

The death of the Peshwā in November 1772 gave rise to disputes regarding the succession to the throne of Pūna. Rāghunāth Rāo, having murdered Mādhu's brother Narāyaṇ Rāo, his own nephew, proclaimed himself Peshwā. The Brāhmaṇ minister, Nāna Farnawīs, and his party declared themselves supporters of the claim of an infant son of Mādhu Rāo. The Bombay Government agreed to maintain Rāghunāth's claim in consideration of the payment of a large sum of money yearly, and the surrender of Salsette and Bassain. The English forces under Colonel Keating defeated the Marāṭhās at Arras, not far from Baroda, and a naval battle was also lost by the latter. The treaty of Puranda left the English in possession of Salsette, and of the revenues of Baroch, while Nāna Farnawīs was recognised as regent at Pūna on payment of a pension to Rāghunāth Rāo. But the war was renewed in 1778. An English force had to make terms in order to secure its retreat from Taligāoñ (Convention of Worgāoñ, 13th January 1779). Early in 1780, however, Colonel Goddard captured Aḥmadābād and inflicted two defeats upon the Marāṭhās. Major Popham at the head of another portion of the Bengal army defeated Sindia and stormed Gwālior. Goddard took Bassain, and Hartley defeated another Marāṭhā force not long afterwards. In March 1781 Colonel Carnal routed Sindia's forces, but Goddard had to retire from the Ghāts with considerable loss.

Meanwhile trouble had arisen with Mysore. Ḥaidar 'Alī had been negotiating with the French, who still held Pondicherri and Mahé. When war broke out between France and England, Pondicherri fell into the Company's hands in October 1778, and Mahé in March 1779. Ḥaidar's army had been drilled by French officers, and was ready for the field. Forming an alliance with the Marāṭhās, Ḥaidar in July 1780 invaded the Carnatic with an immense army, and defeated and utterly destroyed Baillie's column near Conjeveram on the 10th September. Sir Eyre Coote quickly relieved Wandiwash and Chinglipat and captured Karangāli, but suffered a repulse at Chillimboram in June 1781. On the 1st of July, however, with only 8000 men, Coote routed an immense force of the enemy near Kadalor, and in August he won another battle near Conjeveram. Another great victory was won at Sholimgaṛh (27th September). Early next year Coote relieved Vellore, which was besieged by Ḥaidar 'Alī. The Bombay army compelled the enemy to raise the siege of Talicharri after beleaguering it for eighteen months, and took Calicut. But Tippū Sulṭān, son of Ḥaidar 'Alī, defeated and almost exterminated a force of 2000 men under Colonel Braithwaite in Tanjore in that year (1782). Kandalor and Trincomali fell, and Coote's efforts to recover the former place entirely failed. A famine raged around Madras during the same year.

But Hastings had meanwhile been negotiating with some of

the leading Marāṭhā princes, in order to induce them to break off their alliance with Ḥaidar 'Alī. In this he was eminently successful. The Rājā of Birār, Sindia, the Gaikwar, and Nāna Farnawīs made peace with the English; and when Ḥaidar died, in December 1782, Mysore alone carried on the war against the Company.

Tippū Sulṭān, who succeeded his father, was encouraged by the landing of a French force in April 1783, under Bussy. Tippū's troops captured Bednor and Mangalore (January 1784). But peace between France and England had been declared in July 1783, and Tippū was once more left to carry on the contest alone. The Madras Government were, however, weary of the war, and they therefore made a treaty of peace with their formidable foe in March 1784.

Hastings had meanwhile marched against the Rājā of Banāras, Chait Singh, to compel the payment of a subsidy which the Government of Calcutta demanded. Popham captured Bījīgaṛh, and a nephew of the Rājā was put in the latter's place on payment of a larger subsidy than had originally been demanded. Hastings also made a treaty with the Nawâb of Oudh, Asafu'ddaulah, by which the latter was permitted to seize a large amount of property which, rightly or wrongly, was in the possession of the mother and the widow of the late Nawâb, and therewith to pay his debts to the Government of Bengal. Hastings required money in order to carry on the war with Mysore, but his conduct in the matter of the Begams was afterwards one of the items in the impeachment against him before Parliament. It was also one of the reasons why he felt compelled to resign his position and to return home in February 1785. Lord Cornwallis arrived as his successor in 1786.

Tippū Sulṭān again began war at the end of 1789 by attacking Travancore, a State under the protection of the English. The latter formed an alliance with the Niẓām and the Peshwā against him. General Medows advanced from Madras into Mysore and captured Pālghāt, while Colonel Hartley defeated the Mysore army at Calicut, and Abercrombie took Kananor. Bangalore surrendered to Cornwallis in March 1791, and he defeated Tippū at Arikēra on the 14th May the same year, but had to withdraw through want of provisions. Somewhat later Koimbator was captured by Tippū after a gallant defence. In 1792, however, Lord Cornwallis attacked the Mysore capital, Seringapatam, and Tippū was compelled to surrender, losing half of his kingdom, giving two of his sons as hostages, and paying three crores of rupees as war indemnity (19th March). Kūrg, Dindigal, Malabar, and the Baramaḥall were taken by the Company, and portions of the fine and of the conquered territory were given to the native allies of the conquerors.

Meanwhile Sindia had been called to the aid of one of the contending factions at Delhi. He compelled Shāh 'Alam to create the Peshwā regent of the empire, while he himself carried on the government as the Peshwa's deputy. He drilled his army in the European manner, and though for a time in difficulties, owing to the opposition of the Rājpūts and other foes, he defeated his enemies near Âgra in June 1788, and then began to intrigue against the English.

Before his retirement in 1793, Lord Cornwallis had promoted many important internal reforms in Bengal. His successor, Sir John Shore, refused to help the Niẕām in his war with the Peshwā in 1795, in spite of the fact that by the treaty of 1790 the English had bound themselves to do so in case of need. The Peshwā, as head of the league of the whole of the Marāṭhā States, led into the field an army of 130,000 men, while the army of the Niẕām had been trained in the European manner by French officers, and was not far inferior in numbers. In the battle of Kurdla (11th March 1795) the Niẕām was utterly defeated, and obliged to pay three crores of rupees and to surrender a large portion of his territory as the price of peace. But Nana Farnawîs' power was soon after greatly weakened by quarrels about the succession, which ensued upon the suicide of the Peshwā, Mādhu Rāo, in October 1795.

On the death of Asafu'ddaulah in 1797, Sir John Shore, after some hesitation, appointed the late Nawāb-wazîr's brother, Sa'ādat 'Alî, to the throne of Oudh, the latter agreeing to give over Ilāhābād and to maintain 10,000 soldiers of the Company (January 1798). In March Sir John Shore (Lord Teignmouth) went to England, and in May Lord Mornington came out as his successor.

The new Governor-General, on learning that Tippū Sulṯān was intriguing with the French Republic, formed an alliance with the Niẕām against him. The Niẕām dismissed the French officers still in his employ, disbanded his army, and received an English force into Ḥaidārābād (October 1798), where the

English have ever since exercised all real power. The Peshwā and Sindia would not bind themselves to support the Company. Zamān Shāh of Kābul was threatening an incursion into the Panjāb and the territories of the Great Mughul, while Napoleon had landed in Egypt and was planning the overthrow of the English in India. Hence it was necessary to overthrow Tippū ere he received the external aid for which he was eagerly begging. In February 1799, accordingly, the Madras army under General Harris, accompanied by that of the Nizām, advanced into Mysore. The Bombay army from Kananor was commanded by Stuart and Hartley. Tippū attacked Hartley's force on the 6th March, but was repulsed on the arrival of General Stuart. On the 27th he was defeated by Harris at Malavalli and retired towards Seringapatam. Harris, forming a junction of his forces with those advancing from Bombay, crossed the Kāvarī, and on the 17th April laid siege to the enemy's capital. The city was carried by storm on the 3rd of May. Tippū himself fell fighting bravely. A portion of his dominions was reserved for the heir of the Rājā, who had been ousted by Ḥaidar 'Alī when he usurped the throne; of the remainder, part was given to the Niẕām, and the rest was united to the Company's possessions.

In the same year the Governor-General, now created Marquis Wellesley, annexed Tanjore, and soon after Surat and the Carnatic, to the English dominions. In 1800 Captain Malcolm was sent by the Governor-General as envoy to the Shāh of Persia, to engage the latter to hinder Napoleon's threatened advance upon India. The Nawāb of Oudh was in November 1801 compelled to surrender Rohilk'hand, Gorakpūr, and other districts, while in return the English undertook to protect his dominions from the attack which the Marāṭhās, under Sindia, and the Sikhs from the Panjāb, were then threatening. Lord Wellesley's political schemes for the encouragement of trade, the reform of the civil and criminal courts, and other matters of importance, afterwards bore good fruit.

When Nāna Farnawīs died in 1800, dissensions began among the members of the Marāṭhā confederacy. Sindia and Holkar engaged in war with one another. The Peshwā, Bājī Rāo, was obliged to seek the assistance of the English. The treaty of Bassain, in December 1802, bound him to wage no war without the Governor-General's consent. He had been banished from his kingdom, but was replaced on the throne by the English in May 1803. Soon after he began to negotiate with Sindia, who, in alliance with the Rājā of Birār, was threatening to attack him and the English.

War with the Marāṭhās broke out in August of the same year. General Wellesley took Aḥmadnagar on the 12th of that month, and General Lake besieged 'Alīgaṛh at the same time. The battle of Assai, won by Wellesley on the 23rd September, overthrew the Marāṭhā power in the South. Asīrgaṛh soon after fell. 'Alīgaṛh was taken on the 29th August, and Lake then marched against Delhi, which he victoriously entered on the 11th September. Another victory near Âgra in October decided the fate of the latter city. The victory of Lāswārī (1st November) completed the overthrow of Sindia's power. A very large portion of his dominions, including Kattāk, the Doāb (or North-West Provinces), and Baroch, was annexed to the Company's territory. Aḥmadnagar fell to Bājī Rāo, and Western Birār was given to the Niẕām. Rājpūtāna, Sirhind, and Gujarāt were also brought under partial control of the Company.

Holkar now provoked attack, which the monsoon of 1804 for a time prevented from being effectually made. Crossing the Chambal he advanced against Delhi in October, at the head of an army of 20,000 men. General Lake marched from Âgra to the defence of Colonel Ochterlony's small force, which held that city, and Holkar then made an incursion into the Doāb. On 13th November he sustained a defeat at Dhīg, and a few days later another at Farrukhābād. Lake failed to carry Bhartpūr by storm, but the Rājā, who had aided Holkar, soon yielded. Lord Cornwallis again became Governor-General in 1805, but died the same year. The feeble policy of Sir George Barlow (under instructions from home) enabled Holkar and Sindia to regain much of their power; and both the Peshwā and the Niẕām began a course of conduct which almost caused a renewal of the Marāṭhā war.

In July 1806 a Sepoy mutiny broke out at Vellore, but was speedily repressed. Lord Minto became Governor-General in July 1807, and was compelled to take steps to prevent Ranjīt Singh's designs upon Sirhind. War was averted by a treaty made with him in April 1809. Piracy was also largely suppressed in the same year by the acquisition of the ports on the Malabar coast, whence the pirates used to issue forth on their work of destruction. Mauritius and Bourbon were taken from the French in 1810, and Java from the Dutch not long afterwards. A rebellion in Travancore was put down in 1809, and a mutiny among English officers at Seringapatam was also quelled.

When Lord Minto was recalled in 1813, trouble was brewing in Central India, owing to the increasing power of the Pindārīs, a body of mounted robbers who then harried the country. But the first task of his successor, Lord Moira, afterwards created Marquis of Hastings, was to subdue the Gurk'has of Nipāl. Beginning in 1814, the war was not ended until Sir David Ochterlony in 1816 marched on Khatmandū. An English resident was placed at the court of Nipāl, and Kumaun was annexed. The Peshwā was humbled in 1817, and in the same year Hastings advanced against the Pindārīs, who were aided by the Marāṭhās. The robbers were put down, Pūna was taken, and the Peshwā's troops were defeated at Ashtī (19th February 1818). Bājī Rāo surrendered at Indore in May, and his power was brought to an end. The Rājā of Birār was defeated near Nāgpūr, and obliged to take refuge at Ranjīt Singh's court. Holkar's army was routed at Mahidpūr at the end of 1817, and he was obliged to sign a treaty which placed his kingdom under the Company's protection (6th January 1818). This victorious campaign put an end to the Marāṭhā power. Lord Hastings' rule was marked by provision for the education of the native youth, the digging of a canal at Delhi, and other works of great advantage to the country. Java was restored to the Dutch and Singapore purchased in 1819.

Lord Amherst became Governor-General in August 1823. He was obliged to declare war upon Burma in February 1824, through an invasion of Bengal by the Burmese general, Bandūla. The latter was repulsed; Rangoon was captured by Sir Archibald Campbell in May; in April of the next year Donabyū and Prome fell, and Richards had driven the Burmese out of Assam. Morrison's march from Chittagong to Arakān in 1825 was successful, though disease caused the loss of a large portion of his force. Sir A. Campbell's operations in that year compelled the Burmese monarch to submit, surrendering Assam, Arakān, and Tenasserim to the English, and paying one million sterling towards the cost of the war (Treaty of Yandabū, 24th February 1826).

Meanwhile a mutiny among the Sepoys of the 47th Bengal

Infantry had occurred in October 1824. On the 2nd November it was sternly suppressed. War had also occurred with the Rājā of Bhartpūr, but Lord Combermore stormed that fortress on the 18th January 1826. The Rājā was dethroned, his nephew placed on the throne in his stead, and the fortress of Bhartpūr dismantled.

Lord William Bentinck, who succeeded Lord Amherst in 1828, put down *satī* in 1829, and the next year suppressed the Thugs (Ṭhags). He admitted natives to the higher ranks of the Civil Service, altered for the better the laws which pressed most heavily upon native Christians, replaced Persian in the law courts by the use of the native languages, introduced the study of English into the Government colleges, and revised the affairs of the North-West Provinces. Kūrg and Kachār were annexed, and a revolt in Mysore was suppressed.

In 1831 the Wahhābī sect, founded by Sayyid Aḥmad, proclaimed a *Jihād* against the infidels; but this was soon suppressed, as was a disturbance among the Kōls in 1832. The Nairs, K'hōnds, and other savage aboriginal tribes were gradually tamed, and an effort was made to put down the custom of female infanticide among the Rājpūts. The Indus and Satlaj were opened to English commerce through treaties made with Ranjīt Singh and the Amīrs of Sindh.

Lord Auckland became Governor-General in 1836. In 1839 he dethroned the Rājā of Satāra for his intrigues. But his unfortunate Afghān policy brought on a very serious war with that country. Learning that Dost Muḥammad, Amīr of Kābul, was holding negotiations with Russia, Lord Auckland allied himself with Ranjīt Singh in an attempt to dethrone the Amīr and to place Shāh Shujā' on the throne in his stead. The allies entered Kandahār in April 1839, and stormed Ghaznī in July. In August Shāh Shujā' entered Kābul, and the invading force was strengthened in September by the arrival of Colonel Wade's army. Soon after, having placed the new Amīr on the throne, the English and Sikhs retired, leaving Sir W. Macnaughten as political agent at Kābul, with a force of 10,000 men of the Bengal army. In November 1840 Dost Muḥammad surrendered himself prisoner, and was pensioned and sent to India. But the Khiljī tribes revolted in the following year, and, though they were defeated in two battles, the insurrection quickly spread throughout the whole country. Sir Alexander Burnes was murdered in November; and on

11th December the aged General Elphinstone entered into an agreement with Akbar Khān, son of Dost Muḥammad, to withdraw the British army from the country. But during an interview between Macnaughten and Akbar Khān, the latter murdered the English agent (23rd December). General Elphinstone evacuated his cantonments on the 6th January 1842, with his force of 4500 troops, having with him some 12,000 camp followers, besides a number of English women and children. He left four officers as hostages, and abandoned his treasure and almost all his ordnance. In defiance of the treaty, the Afghāns attacked the retiring force, which had also to contend against the severe cold of an Afghān winter. Only one man, Dr. Brydon, survived to reach Jalālābād and tell the dismal tale, all the others perishing, except about 120 prisoners taken by Akbar Khān and afterwards rescued. But Nott and Rawlinson at Kandahār, and Sale at Jalālābād, bravely held their positions, in spite of every effort of the enemy to overpower them. Sale stood a siege of five months' duration, and then marched out and defeated the Afghāns. General Polluck soon afterwards fought his way through the Khaibar Pass and relieved him (15th April). In August Nott advanced from Kandahār and Polluck from Jalālābād. They defeated the enemy at Ghaznī, Tazīn, and other places, and on the 16th September the Bālā Ḥiṣār at Kābul was again in the possession of an English army. The surviving captives were rescued by Sir Richmond Shakespear before the end of the month. The English destroyed the great bāzār at Kābul. They pillaged the city, and then, on the 12th October, began their march back to India. Shah Shujā' had been murdered by the people upon whom he had unwillingly been forced by foreign arms. Dost Muḥammad was set free and recovered his throne; and the result of the war, which had cost so much blood and treasure, was to render the Afghāns more decidedly hostile than ever.

Meanwhile Lord Auckland had been succeeded by Lord Ellenborough in February 1842. Just before his retirement, however, Lord Auckland had been induced to do two good deeds, which removed a long-continued scandal. The connection between the Government and the maintenance of the Hindū temples with their foul rites was abolished, and the Company's troops were no longer required to show idolatrous reverence on the occasion of Hindū festivals.

The first Sindh War broke out early in 1843. Sir Charles

Napier advanced up the Indus to Ḥaidarābād with a force of 2600 men. At Miānī near that city he was met by a force of 26,000 infantry and 10,000 cavalry. A terrible and hardly contested battle on the 17th February resulted in a victory for the English, which cost their opponents the loss of 6000 men. Next day Ḥaidarābād surrendered. Napier, having received reinforcements, fought another battle at Dabha on the 24th, defeating Shīr Muḥammad's army of 26,000 men. The whole country was then annexed to the Bombay Presidency, Sir Charles Napier being appointed governor of the territory he had won.

A war with the Marāṭhā State of Gwālior began in December 1843. It was soon ended by the victories gained at Mahārājpūr and Paniār, and Colonel Sleeman, the English resident, was intrusted with the virtual control of the Council of Regency which was appointed to govern the country.

Before Lord Ellenborough's retirement in 1844 slavery had been abolished in British India, and a mutiny among the Bengal Sepoys had been suppressed.

Sir Henry Hardinge had to put down a rebellion among the Marāṭhās at Kolāpūr in October 1844; and a short campaign in 1845 overthrew the Bilochīs, who had invaded Sindh. But the long threatened war with the Sikhs was begun in December the same year, when the army of the Khālsā or Sikh league, to the number of 60,000 men, crossed the Satlaj and encamped before Fīrūzpūr. On the 18th December Sir Hugh Gough was attacked at Mudkī by 20,000 of the enemy. After a fierce struggle the Sikhs were routed. A still more severe contest took place a few days later at Fīrūzshahr, where Gough's force of 17,000 men was confronted by an army of at least 40,000 Sikhs. The contest lasted for the greater part of two days (21st and 22nd December 1845), and the victory cost the English over 2400 men.

In January 1846 the Sikhs under Ranjor Singh crossed the Satlaj and laid siege to Ludhiāna. Sir H. Smith relieved the city, and then defeated the enemy at Aliwāl, eight miles off. The Sikhs strongly fortified themselves at Sobrāōn, where Gough, on the 10th February with 15,000 men, attacked their force of 35,000 men, and, after one of the most fiercely fought battles of the whole war, defeated them with great loss. No fewer than 10,000 Sikhs fell on the field or perished in the pursuit; but the victors lost almost 2400 men. The road to the Sikh capital, Lahore, then lay open. A treaty was signed on the 23rd February by the ministers of the Rājā, Dhulīp Singh, who was a minor. Jalandhar and the Sikh territory on the left bank of the Satlaj were surrendered to the Company, and a large war indemnity was promised. In order to pay this, Kashmīr was soon afterwards sold to Gûlâb Singh of Jammū. Lahore was restored to the Sikhs, but their army was disbanded.

The rest of the period of Lord Hardinge's rule was mostly devoted to the suppression of infanticide and slavery in the native States, to digging the Ganges Canal, and to promoting education.

Lord Dalhousie succeeded him in 1848. He endeavoured to supersede Mulrāj, the Sikh governor of Multān, and to appoint in his place one on whose fidelity the Government could better rely. Mulrāj murdered the two officers intrusted with this hazardous duty; but he was defeated and shut up in Multān by Lieutenant Herbert Edwardes. A general revolt of the Sikhs followed. General Whish stormed Multān; and Mulrāj, who bravely held out in the citadel until it was no longer tenable, surrendered at discretion on the 22nd January 1849. Lord Gough encountered the Sikhs at Chiliānwālā on the 13th January, and compelled them to retreat; but the battle was almost a drawn one. Another battle at Gujarāt on the 21st February ended in the defeat of the enemy. The remnants of their army surrendered at Rāwal Piṇḍī on the 11th March. The Panjāb was annexed to the British Empire on the 29th March 1849. Dhulīp Singh became a pensioner of the Company. Sir Henry Lawrence, to whom the management of the new province was intrusted, succeeded so well in winning the hearts of the people that they remained unshaken in their allegiance to their new rulers even in the terrible times of the Mutiny, and they have ever since supplied some of the bravest and most trustworthy of our Indian troops.

The second Burmese War broke out in 1852. It was occasioned by ill-treatment inflicted on English residents at Ava, and by an assault on an English frigate at Rangoon. An English fleet bombarded and captured that city in April. Bassain fell in May, and Pegu in June of that year. Donabyū was captured early in 1853, and the war ended with the annexation of Pegu (June 1853).

In 1848 Satāra was annexed, Birār and Jhānsī in 1853, and Oudh in 1856. Before Lord Dalhousie left India in March of the latter year, he had introduced extensive improvements into the administration of Indian affairs. Telegraphs, railways, a half-anna postage, and irrigation canals in the Panjāb and in other places were among the gains made by the country during his term of government. His successor, Lord Canning, sent an army to Bushire, in order to compel the Shāh of Persia to desist from his attack upon Herāt. Bushire was easily taken by General Outram (December 1856). He routed the Persian army at Khūshāb on the 8th February 1857, and took Muhammarah on the 26th March. The war ended soon after. The Shāh withdrew his troops from Herāt, which was left in possession of Dost Muḥammad, with whom Sir John Lawrence entered into a treaty of alliance in January 1857.

It was in that year that the ever memorable Indian Mutiny broke out. It would take too long to dwell on its real or supposed causes, to deal with the question of the greased cartridges, and to decide who were the most deeply guilty among the leaders in the revolt, which for the moment united both Hindū and Muḥammadan Sepoys against the English government of the country. Nor is it necessary to dwell long on the fearful details of the many massacres which followed one another so quickly in different parts of the country. The history of the Mutiny and its suppression has been most fully and graphically written by able historians. After a few isolated outbreaks, which were put down without difficulty, the Mutiny began at Mīraṭh on the 10th May 1857. The 3rd Bengal Cavalry in that city rose, murdered their officers and all other Europeans whom they could find, and then marched to Delhi. There a fearful massacre of all the English residents took place. Willoughby and his small band of comrades in charge of the magazine there blew it up to prevent it from falling into the mutineers' hands. The mutiny spread throughout the greater part of Hindūstān proper, and similar scenes of courage and massacre were again and again repeated. The cities of Âgra, Jalālābād, and Banāras were retained by their English garrisons. Our few troops at Cawnpore and Lucknow were besieged. The massacre of nearly 900 men, women, and children at Cawnpore by the orders of Nāna Ṣāḥib, Rājā of Bit'hūr, on the 15th July, will ever live in the memory of Englishmen. Havelock's capture of the city was just too late to save them.

His relief of Lucknow was hindered for a time, in spite of two brave attempts which he made to reach that city, by the smallness of his force and the large number of the enemy. At last, Havelock, Outram, and Neill, with great loss, storming the 'Ālambāgh, forced their way through to the Residency on the 25th September, and relieved its gallant defenders from immediate danger, though their rescue was not completed until the arrival of Sir Colin Campbell's army on the 17th November.

Meanwhile a small band of heroes had held the historic ridge overlooking Delhi, the centre of the revolt. They were too few to lay siege to the city, nay rather, they were themselves besieged by the overwhelming masses of the enemy. At last, General Nicholson, with all the troops which could possibly be spared from the Panjāb, arrived to reinforce them, and the city was finally besieged on the 6th September. Troops were hurried forward from all quarters, and an entrance was effected on the 14th of that month. But it still required six days' contest in the streets before the city was captured. Its fall sealed the fate of the Mughul dynasty. The old king, Muḥammad Bahādur Shāh, was condemned to death, but his sentence was commuted to imprisonment in Pegu. Next year the mutineers were overthrown in Oudh, Rohilk'hand, and Gwālior, and the whole country again brought into subjection to the English.

The Mutiny brought the rule of the East India Company to an end. The Queen's proclamation, announcing that the government of India had been transferred to the Crown, was read by Lord Canning at a great *darbār* held at Ilāhābād on the 1st November 1858. Lord Canning was appointed the first Viceroy of India, and with his assumption of that office a new epoch in the history of the country began.

CHAPTER VI

FROM THE SUPPRESSION OF THE MUTINY TO THE PRESENT TIME.

One of the most important paragraphs in the Queen's Proclamation was that in which, while acknowledging the Christian Faith as her own, she pledged her word to respect the beliefs of all her Indian subjects. Thus for the first time in India were religious equality and religious liberty established on a firm and permanent basis, and Christian missionaries were henceforth enabled to work without being liable to hindrance from the English government of the country. The Penal Code drawn up by Macaulay became law in 1860. When the Viceroy's Legislative Council was remodelled in 1861, native princes were rendered eligible for admission as members, and the Rājā of Patiāla was the first of them thus admitted. Patents were issued to feudatory princes to adopt heirs in case of need. A High Court of Judicature was appointed, and native judges were permitted to qualify for admission to membership.

In 1861 a great famine broke out in Upper India, and caused about 500,000 deaths. Lord Canning's successor in 1862 was Lord Elgin, who, however, died at Dharmsāla in November 1863. During his brief tenure of office the Sitāna campaign had begun. General Neville Chamberlain's advance into the Ambēla Pass was hotly contested by the mountaineers, but reinforcements arrived which enabled Garnock, his successor, to carry Ambēla by storm in December 1863. The destruction of Malka soon afterwards brought the war to a successful termination. Sir William Denison acted as Viceroy until Sir John Lawrence, in January 1864, assumed the reigns of government. The Bhotan campaign, which began in November of that year and was ended in 1865, was followed by the Black Mountain Expedition of 1868. In the same year Shīr 'Alī

Khān, one of the sons of Dost Muḥammad, succeeded in seating himself on the throne of Kābul after a civil war in Afghānistān.

Sir William Temple and Sir Arthur Phayre, as governors of the Central Provinces and of British Burma respectively, worked well and successfully for the encouragement of trade and the general well-being of those districts. The same may be said of the rule of Sir Robert Montgomery and Sir Donald M'Leod in the Panjāb. The Ganges canal, with its numerous branches, in large measure prevented a famine in the districts watered by it in 1868. Rājpūtāna, however, suffered severely in that year, though not so severely as Orissa had done from the famine of 1866. The extension of railways greatly increased commerce, while the irrigation works in many different parts of the country increased the productiveness of the land, and enabled it to support the steady increase of population. Sanitation was cared for by municipal committees, and the work of educating the people, begun by the missionaries, was largely undertaken by the State.

Lord Mayo, who became Viceroy in 1869, at a *darbār* held at Ambāla in March of the same year, began the policy of paying an annual subsidy to the Amīr of Afghānistān and supplying him with arms in order to enable him to resist Russian aggression. This policy is still maintained by the Government of India. Another serious mistake made by Lord Mayo was the great increase in the Income Tax, which caused widespread oppression and discontent.

An incursion into Kachār in January 1871 rendered the Loshai Expedition (November 1871 to February 1872) necessary. Many important administrative reforms marked Lord Mayo's tenure of the Viceroyalty. He was murdered by a convict in the Andaman Islands on the 8th February 1872. Lord Northbrook took his place in May of the same year. In March 1873 he abolished the hated Income Tax. His talents as a financier bore good fruit in Indian affairs. By means of the relief works which he instituted in Bengal, he largely assisted in mitigating the horrors of the famine that raged in that province in 1874. The Gaikwar of Baroda was dethroned in 1875 for disloyalty and persistent misgovernment of his dominions. That year and the next are memorable for the visit of our present King, then the Prince of Wales, to India.

Lord Lytton became Viceroy in 1876. The same year a

great famine broke out in Southern India and lasted until 1878. It was widespread in its ravages, and was one of the worst on record since the establishment of British rule in the country. Queen Victoria was proclaimed Empress of India by the Persian title of *Qaiṣar i Hind* at a great *darbār* near Delhi on the 1st January 1877, in accordance with a Bill passed in Parliament on Mr. Disraeli's motion the preceding year.

An Afghān war broke out in 1878. Shīr 'Alī the Amīr had become alarmed at the Russian conquests in Central Asia, and, finding that he could not obtain adequate assistance from England, he began to negotiate with Russia. He received a Russian Embassy with great honour into his capital, and refused to admit one from the Indian Government. An ultimatum was sent to the Amīr, and, as no answer was received, three British columns entered Afghānistān by the Khaibar, the Kurām, and the Bolan Passes respectively. The 'Alī Masjid fort was carried by General Browne's column, while that under General Roberts' command fought a battle at Paiwār Kutal and drove the enemy in headlong flight to Kābul. General Stewart's force reached Kandahār without much opposition. The Amīr fled to Turkistān and died there. His son and successor, Ya'qūb Khān, concluded a treaty at Gandamak with Sir S. Browne, in virtue of which our frontier was extended beyond the three passes, the possession of which was necessary for the protection of India from invasion from the North. It was also agreed that a British Mission should be received at Kābul.

Sir Louis Cavagnari was sent to the Amīr's court, accompanied by only a handful of men. At first they were well received. They were attacked by the Amīr's Herātī troops on the night of the 2nd September 1879, and all fell after a desperate resistance.

This necessitated a second Afghān war. General Roberts advanced through the Kurām Valley, and the Amīr came to his camp and was made prisoner, being unable to clear himself of the charge of complicity in the recent massacre. General Roberts gained a brilliant victory over a large Afghān army which in vain endeavoured to bar the way to Kābul. Kābul was occupied; the Amīr resigned his crown, and was sent as a prisoner to India.

When winter set in, General Roberts' force was fiercely attacked, and ultimately obliged to retire to the camp at

Shirpūr (December 1879). A repulse on the night of the 22nd December, and the arrival of reinforcements from Jalālābād next day, completed the discomfiture of the enemy. Early next year General Stewart advanced from Kandahār, defeating 15,000 Afghāns at Aḥmad Khel after a desperate struggle, in which both sides lost heavily. He took Ghaznî, and reached Kābul in May 1880.

'Abdu'rraḥmān Khān meanwhile became Amîr, and was recognised by the British Government. Our troops were just about to retire from Kābul and return to India when news reached them of the disaster which had befallen General Burrows' force at Maiwand, fifty miles from Kandahār. The late Amîr's brother, Ayyūb Khān, governor of Herāt, attacked the British force at Maiwand and defeated them (27th July 1880). It was with great difficulty that the survivors of a force of 2000 men managed to make good their retreat to Kandahār, where they were besieged by Ayyūb Khān's army. But General Roberts pressed on to Kandahār with an army of 10,000 men, and reached the city in nineteen days, after one of the most famous marches in history. On the 1st September he routed Ayyūb's army, capturing his camp and all his artillery. Our forces then returned to India, leaving 'Abdu'rraḥmān, who had assisted us to some extent against his rival, in peaceful possession of the throne. He has ever since preserved friendly relations with the Indian Government, with whom he has formed a defensive alliance.

The Marquis of Ripon became Viceroy in the same year (1880). Under him and his successors, the Marquis of Dufferin, Lord Lansdowne, Lord Elgin, and Lord Curzon the present Viceroy, the country has made steady progress. There have occurred no wars of great importance, the principal being the Chitral and Wazîri expeditions. The whole of Burma has been annexed, King Theebau's cruelties having rendered his deposition necessary. The Indian Government have not yet ceased to encourage the cultivation of opium and the opium trade with China, one of the greatest blots upon our Eastern Empire. The plague, which has now raged for four years in India, in spite of the utmost efforts of the Government to check its progress, seems to have become endemic. The famine of 1899–1900 was one far exceeding in severity any other on record since India was united to the British Crown. Yet in spite of the terrible mortality thus produced, the population of

British India amounted at the end of the nineteenth century to the enormous number of 294,266,701.

In this brief *résumé* of the history of India nothing is more remarkable than the marvellous manner in which the British Empire in that country arose and has extended its bounds, often unwillingly, until the whole country has become subject to the British Crown. If we believe as much as the heathen king Nebuchadnezzar did after his experience of God's dealings with him, we must acknowledge that "The Most High [1] ruleth in the kingdom of men, and giveth it to whomsoever He will." For what purpose then has He given us India? Is it not that, by making due provision for the physical, mental, moral, and spiritual benefit of its people, we may be workers together with Him, and hasten the day when they shall turn from their false religions to serve with us the living God, and to wait for His Son from heaven, who came to seek and to save that which was lost?

[1] Dan. iv. 17.

PART II

THE RELIGIONS OF INDIA

CHAPTER I

HINDŪISM.

HINDŪISM, from its complexity and multiformity, and from the frequently contradictory tenets taught by the innumerable sects who are all included under the national rather than religious appellation of *Hindūs*, is perhaps of all religions the most difficult to describe and explain within the limits of a few pages. During its long period of development it has shown a marvellous power of absorbing religious ideas from all or almost all possible quarters. It has traces of the teaching of the Vedas, which indeed may be said to form its substratum. But it has also absorbed the doctrines of many different schools of philosophy ranging from Deism to Atheism, those of the aborigines of India, the teachings of Buddha and his followers, and perhaps something of Muḥammadan and of Christian tenets also. The only connecting link which binds together in one the various sects into which Hindūism is divided is the system of *Caste*, which, though it has no real foundation in the Vedic Hymns and formed no part of the early religious system of the Indian Āryans, now dominates all Hindūs alike, from the highest to the lowest. Caste holds sway over family, religious, and business life equally, and is to-day the most distinguishing feature of the religion of the Hindūs.

We proceed to give a short sketch of Hindūism as it exists in the India of to-day, following as far as possible the historical course of its growth and development.

When the Âryans, leaving their ancestral home in the region encircling the modern city of Herāt, which the Avestā entitles the "Âryan abode," entered India in the second millennium before Christ, they brought with them a system of religion, not as yet fully formulated, but which in its general features must have greatly resembled the faiths which we find ages after in Hellas, Italy and Scandinavia. This may be briefly described as Nature-worship. The whole universe seemed to be pervaded by superhuman beings, mostly of benignant disposition, though some among them were malignant. The latter, however, though feared, were not entitled to worship. The word which in the Sanskṛit tongue signifies a god, *Deva*, is derived from the root *div*, "to shine," and hence originally meant a bright, a shining one. The Greeks retained the same word as Θεός, and the Romans in the forms *Deus* and *Divus*. One of the most ancient Âryan conceptions was that of *Dyaush-pitā*, "Heaven-Father," the same in name and in nature as the Ζεὺς πατήρ of Hellas, the *Iovis Pater* (*Iuppiter*) of Rome, and the *Tiu* of ancient Germany. The story contained in the Eddas of Scandinavia, which relates how the giant Ymir was slain, and how the earth and the heavens were formed from his remains, is also to be found in the Ṛig-Veda,[1] told there of *Purusha*, the primaeval male. The Roman *Mars* was the Indian *Mṛityu*, God of Death, in Pālī *Māro*. This and much more we learn from comparative Philology and Religion.

The oldest literary productions of the Âryan race which have been preserved for us are the Hymns of the Ṛig-Veda. That work is believed to have been composed, though not yet written down, between 1500 and 1000 years before our era. In it we already find something closely resembling the *pantheistic* conceptions which now form the basis of all Hindūism. Pantheism, in fact, seems to be the leading doctrine of the Âryan or Japhetic race, as Monotheism is that of the Semitic, and Metempsychosis that of the other great race of the Old World, to which we may apply the Biblical term Hamitic. But the Four Vedas preserve for us not only in Dyaush-pitā, but still more perhaps in *Varuṇa* (the Οὐρανός of Greece), distinct traces of an earlier belief in a Heavenly Father, which grew fainter and was gradually lost amid the thickening mists of heathenism. Besides Varuṇa we find many other deities worshipped by the ancient Âryans in India, the chief of whom were *Agni* (*Ignis*)

[1] Ṛig-Veda, x. 90.

or Fire, and *Soma*, the intoxicating juice of the plant of the same name. *Indra*, the god of the atmosphere, was their national deity, the giver of victory to his people, the wielder of the thunderbolt. *Vishṇu* is his comrade, and the *Maruts* or Storm-gods are his bodyguard. *Rudra*, the father of these latter, is closely related to *Vāyu* or *Vāta*, the wind, and *Parjanya*, the rain-storm. *Bṛihaspati* or *Brahmaṇaspati*, "the lord of prayer," is sometimes identified with Agni and more frequently with Indra. *Sûrya*, the Sun, *Ushas*, the Dawn, *Aditi*, Immensity, mother of the *Ādityas* (who resemble the classical Διοσκοῦροι), *Tvashtā*, the fashioner, who made the thunderbolts of Indra, just as Hephaestus or Vulcan did those of Zeus or Jupiter, and many other divine beings, meet with us in the Vedic Hymns. *Yama*, son of the Sun, might have lived immortal, but chose to die, and was the first to travel along the dark path of death. Hence he is king of the realms of the dead, and gathers round him the *Pitṛis*, or fathers, who have lived worthily, and who now, rendered immortal by drinking the *soma*-juice, the *amṛita* or *ambrosia*, sit at the table of the gods and share in their worship.

The Indian Âryans attributed sex to their deities, and held that the Golden Germ (*Hiraṇya-garbha*) was the source from which all things sprang. But they did not indulge in the obscene religious practices to which such ideas have since given rise among their descendants. Their gods worked for the establishment of truth (*satya*) and order (*ṛita*). Hymns and sacrifices of different kinds were offered to them, especially those of the horse, bull, cow, buffalo, goat, ram; but offerings of clarified butter (the modern *ghī*), *soma*-juice, and cakes were also frequently made.

Max Müller describes their religion as *Henotheism*, because, though worshipping at least the thirty-three Vedic deities, they frequently clothed each of their deities in turn with all the divine attributes, thus seeming tacitly to acknowledge the Oneness of the Divine, and approaching Monotheism though not attaining it.

All this religion has long been a thing of the past in India; but, as it forms the germ from which later Hindūism has been evolved, and as modern attempts to reform Hindūism profess to restore the worship of Vedic times, it is necessary for the student of Hindūism to know the main outline of that system, if system it can be called, before proceeding to study its later developments.

In the course of time, when the old language of the Vedas gradually became obsolete and was changed into the classical Sanskṛit and into the various Prâkṛit or vulgar dialects, the religion of Vedic times underwent very material changes. One reason for this was doubtless the influence exercised over the mass of the Âryan population by the Drâviḍian, Kolarian, and aboriginal tribes, who formed the lower strata of society, but must have vastly outnumbered the Âryan immigrants, except perhaps in the Panjāb, where were the earliest Âryan settlements in India. The old deities for the most part little by little fell into the background, while new impersonations took their places. In what may be fitly called the Brâhmaṇic period, when the various books known as the Brâhmaṇas were written, *Prajâpati*, the Lord of creatures, becomes recognised as the chief of the gods, and we find the first of the Hindū triads, consisting of Agni, Vâyu and Sûrya, coming to the fore. At the same time the personification of their various attributes led to a great and steady increase in the number of the gods. The pious man, instead of longing to go to Yama's realm, now looked forward to his entrance into *Svarga*, the heaven of Indra. The wicked will go to one of the hells, or else will be reincarnated in some miserable condition. The doctrine of transmigration here first occurs in Sanskṛit writings, and was probably borrowed from the older inhabitants of India. The word *Asura*—originally used in a good sense and denoting a divine being, identical perhaps with the Ahurâo Mazdâo of the Avestā—now came to denote, in the plural, a race of demons, whose contests with the gods (*devas*) are frequently spoken of. Varuṇa himself becomes the god of night, chief of the powers of darkness, and is regarded as cruel and malignant. The worship of *Śiva* becomes developed. The theory of the diverse origin of the four castes, Brâhmaṇs, Kshatriyas, Vaiśyas and Śûdras, is found only in one of the very latest hymns of the Ṛig-Veda,[1] but we now discover it in full operation. The Brâhmaṇ alone has the right to celebrate most of the religious rites which have continued to be observed from ancient times, but he is obliged to repeat the prayers in the manner that has become stereotyped. The religion depicted in the Brâhmaṇas has become formal and lifeless. Many tales are told of the gods, which seem to show in them an entire lack of all moral sense. Ritual has become of the very first importance, and the efficacy of each ceremony is

[1] Ṛig-Veda, x. 90, 11, 12.

due to something magical in its very nature, particularly in the *mantras* or verses which are repeated at the time of its performance. Only somewhat later, in the Sûtras, it is taught that the moral virtues are necessary, as well as the offering of sacrifice, in order to obtain entrance into heaven. There is no public worship, but the Brâhmaṇ performs sacrifices for the devotee. The Brâhmaṇ must also scrupulously perform the private devotions which are incumbent upon pious persons. The most important of these necessary observances was the investiture of every "twice-born" (*dvija*) man (or man of one of the three—the original Âryan—upper castes) with the sacred thread. This constituted his "second birth," after which he became responsible for his acts. For women, for Śūdras, and the other still lower castes which were gradually formed, there was no initiation. Certain daily prayers had to be offered and certain ceremonies performed, especially funeral rites, upon which the happiness of the dead depended. When he grew old, the twice-born man was bound to hand over the care of his family to his eldest son and retire into solitude, in order to prepare for the next world. A moral code, from which ultimately proceeded the various *Dharma-śâstras* or Law Books, was gradually formulated.

There were in Brâhmaṇical times a great number of different kinds of sacrifices, many of which required hecatombs of victims. Priest and worshipper drank the *soma*-juice, of which the god to whom it was offered was also supposed to partake. Human sacrifices were prescribed as necessary at all the great *somayúgas* or sacred feasts at which the juice of the *soma* was drunk. This terrible custom may have been learned by the Âryans in India itself, though we know that it was found among their brethren in Greece, Rome and Britain also in ancient times. Gradually a feeling of the sacredness of all life began to grow up in India, which caused rice and other bloodless offerings to be substituted for victims. At last it became established that a gift to the Brâhmaṇs was better than the offering of any sacrifice whatever. But the inhuman institution of widow-burning (generally called by Europeans *satî*, which term is properly applied to the unfortunate woman who thus immolated herself), of which we find no clear indication in Vedic times, now first comes under notice. This practice was certainly an ancient one, however,[1] for the Greeks found it in use in Alexander's time in at least

[1] Strabo, XV. i. 30.

one tribe in the Panjāb. It seems to have been in vogue particularly, if not solely, among the Kshatriyas at first, but it must have been contrary to the original habits of the Âryans. Not till 1829 was it finally abolished by the orders of Lord William Bentinck.[1] In Vedic times widows were permitted to marry again on certain conditions.

Neither the Vedic nor the Brāhmaṇical worship seems to have required or provided for the use of images or of definitely fixed shrines or holy places. Yet there can be little doubt that from very early times these were to be found in India, much as they are at the present day. But this may be due to their being adopted by the Âryans from the non-Âryan population. The probability of this is strengthened by the fact that the Brâhmaṇs were by the Laws of Manu forbidden to officiate in connection with idols and temples. We find in the times of which we now speak neither pilgrimages nor especially holy places.

While the Brâhmaṇs had the monopoly of the ritual and of the outward part of religion, they were by no means permitted to claim an exclusive right to ponder philosophical questions. At the present time in India a man may practically think and often say what he pleases, but the slightest infringement of the established rites and ancestral customs or practices connected with Caste is a deadly offence. In Brâhmaṇical times it was much the same. Hence arose the six great systems of Indian Philosophy, of which the principal are the *Sânkhya* and the *Vedânta*. In some of them the doctrine of a Personal God, distinct from the world which He governs, was formulated; but the Indian mind does not seem ever to have reached the height at which the Hebrew Scriptures begin, in teaching the existence of one Almighty Creator. In the Bhagavadgîta and the Vedântasâra we are taught that the visible world has no real existence; it exists only in our imagination, or rather in that of the Divine Being, who alone *is*. All else is Mâyâ, "illusion," a "play which the Absolute plays with[2] himself." The Sânkhya philosophy gradually adopted the same belief, though using different technical phrases. The human spirit and human personality are but parts of the "illusion," and the conviction that we exist as distinct from the[3] Absolute Spirit

[1] *The Religions of India*, Eng. ed. p. 60. [2] *Op. cit.* p. 75.

[3] Often in the Upanishads called Brahmâ, and identified with Prajâpati.

is the cause of all moral as well as mental error. "Ignorant[1] of its true nature, the soul attaches itself to objects unworthy of it. Every act which it performs to gratify this attachment entangles it deeper in the perishable world; and, as it is itself imperishable, it is condemned to a perpetual series of changes. Once dragged into the *saṃsâra*, into the vortex of life, it passes from one existence into another, without respite and without rest." The deeds which a man has done, good or bad, bear fruit in the next life, and cause his birth into some other state of existence. This idea had fully taken root in the popular mind before Buddha arose in the sixth century before Christ.

When the human spirit realises its identity and union with the divine, when the soul is absorbed again into that from which it came, the man is "emancipated" from existence. In order to attain that end, it is necessary to stifle all desire and to become weaned from all attachment to earth. Hence, even in Alexander's time ascetics were found in the Panjāb, who with this object inflicted upon themselves tortures very much of the same kind as are still the custom in India among devotees of various sects.

As Brâhmaṇism declined and more corrupt forms of religion gradually absorbed it, until it altogether vanished in Modern Hindūism, various beliefs which are now general in India seem to have come into prominence. One of these is the theory of the successive developments and destructions of the visible universe at the end of great *Kalpas* or world-cycles, another the legend of the four ages[2] of the world. The gods, too, in the popular conception became lowered, and men began to believe that by penances, austerities and sacrifices they might lay up such a store of merit as to become superior to the deities themselves. The practice of making pilgrimages to holy places, and of washing away one's sins by bathing in the Ganges, grew up, and at the present time prevails to an immense extent. Great sacrifices continued to be offered until nearly, or perhaps quite up to, the time of the Muḥammadan conquest of a great part of Hindūstān; but Brâhmaṇism since that time has merged into Hindūism through less and less importance being attached to the old ritual observances. In their places, though doubtless greatly affected by them, the chameleon-like forms of

[1] *Op. cit.* p. 77.

[2] This, however, must have been an original Âryan belief, as its existence among the Greeks and Romans proves.

Modern Hindūism established themselves. Thus we find that, in spite of all the thinkers and philosophers of the past (and of the present too), the course of religion in India has been steadily downward, until the comparatively noble conceptions introduced by the ancient Âryan conquerors have been swallowed up and forgotten in the base and degrading superstitions of the conquered races and in others of more modern origin.

Modern Hindūism rests upon a belief in Pantheism. The creed of India to-day is summed up in the words *Ekam advitiyam*, "One being, without a second." Belief in a deity apart from the world constitutes a heresy, that of the *dvaitas*. Even the most uneducated of the people, though they sometimes speak of "God" as the old Romans and Greeks did, in a manner that would lead a person who had not investigated the subject to fancy that they were Deists or even Monotheists, yet when asked about their faith, state that they are themselves parts of the Deity,[1] as are all other beings in the universe. Another distinguishing feature of Hindūism is the deification of the reproductive powers, as evidenced by the extensive use of the *linga* and *yoni* emblems. In this respect the state of India to-day reminds us forcibly of the corruptions of Baal and Ashtoreth worship among the Babylonians and Phœnicians of antiquity. Each male deity is accompanied by at least one female counterpart. The Mahâbhârata, the Râmâyana, the Prem-sâgar and other books which have superseded the Vedas in the estimation of the people (at least in practice, if not in theory), amply illustrate this, as do the various Purāṇas and Tantras. The *hierodouloi* and their female equivalents of antiquity have abundant representatives in India to-day. This is a subject upon which we do not purpose to dwell, but it is necessary to point this out in order that it may be understood that the abominations of heathenism, so far from being overdrawn, are in reality far worse than can be described by a Christian.

The multitude of Hindū sects existing at the present time

[1] The Deity, as distinct from the many gods and goddesses of modern India, is regarded by the Hindūs as impersonal and neuter. Under ordinary circumstances a Hindū believes that he has to undergo 84,000 transmigrations before he can be absorbed into this impersonal Being, who is at once good and evil, or neither, and lose all consciousness of personality. This weary journey may, however, be shortened by ascetic practices and by intense meditation on the identity of the *âtmâ* and the *paramâtmâ*, etc.

may be broadly subdivided into two great classes, Šivaite and Vishṇuite, according as their members adhere to the worship of Šiva or to that of Vishṇu. Šiva may practically be said to have been developed from the Rudra of the Veda. He is the master of life and death, but the attributes of dread and horror in his character are most to be noticed at the present day. He has three eyes, one in the middle of the forehead, and from this there will one day dart forth the fire which must burn up the world at the end of the present cycle. He is therefore the god of destruction, and is propitious to robbers, brigands, beggars, and religious mendicants. He dwells in forests and desolate places, and especially in the mountains. Among his numerous other titles, he is perhaps best known in modern India as *Mahādeo*, "the great God."

"He[1] sits enthroned on Kailâsa, the fabulous mountain of the North, beyond Himavat (Himālaya), surrounded and waited on by the *Yakshas*, and a great number of spirits of different forms, who receive their orders from his adopted son Skanda, the god of war, and the fosterchild of the Pleiades: from *Ganeśa*, 'the chief of the troops,' the god with the elephant's head, the inspirer of cunning devices and good counsel, afterwards the patron of letters and of learned men; from *Kubera*, the god of treasures; from *Vîrabhadra*, 'the venerable hero,' the personification of fury in battle, whose cultus is widespread in the Dakhan, and who is regarded at times as a form of Šiva himself. His birth is variously represented, but in reality he is eternal; he is *Mahâkâla*, endless time, which begets and devours all things. As procreator, his symbols are the bull and the phallus, as well as the moon, which serves for his diadem. As destroyer, he is clothed in terrible forms; he is armed with the trident, and wears a necklace of skulls. He is identified with *Mṛityu*, Death; and his old surname, *Paśupati*, 'Lord of herds,' acquires the ominous meaning of 'Master of human cattle,' perhaps that of 'Master of victims,' for he is, more than any god, cruel, and exacts a bloody cultus. He is the chief of the *Bhûtas*, of the *Piśâchas*, of mischievous spirits, of ghouls and vampires that frequent places of execution and those where the dead are buried, and he prowls about with them at nightfall. There is an orgiastic side to his nature: he is *Bhairava*, the god of mad, frantic folly, who, clothed in the bloodstained skin of an elephant, leads the wild dance of the

[1] *The Religions of India*, pp. 164, 165.

tāṇḍava. But he is also, *par excellence*, the god of asceticism and austerities. He is the chief of the Yōgîs; like them he goes naked, his body smutty with ashes, his long hair plaited and gathered up in a knot on the crown of his head. The legends are full of his appalling mortifications, and they relate how, with a single glance of his Cyclop eye, he reduced to ashes *Kâma*, Cupid, who had dared to bring trouble into his breast. By his side sits enthroned *Umā*, 'the gracious,' the daughter of Himavat, whom we met with already in some Vedic passages as the wife of Rudra. . . . Like her husband, of whom she is the exact counterpart, she has many names, and assumes many forms. She is worshipped as *Devî*, 'the goddess,' *Pârvatî*, 'the daughter of the mountains,' *Durgâ*, 'the inaccessible,' *Gaurî*, 'the bright one,' *Satî*, 'the devoted wife,' *Bhairavî*, 'the terror-inspiring,' *Kâlî*, 'the black one,' *Karâlâ*, 'the horrible one,' and under no end of other designations, which express her twofold nature as goddess of life and goddess of death."

The murderous set of the *Thugs* (*Ṭhags*), long the terror of India, who used to waylay travellers, and, having made friendship with them, unexpectedly strangle them, were devotees of Kâlî, and in this manner used to propitiate their cruel goddess with human sacrifices.

The modern worship of *Vishṇu* (an old Vedic god, but not then regarded as of much importance) seems to have reached its present height through his being identified by the Brâhmaṇs with *Kṛishṇa*, who was probably the clan-god of a combination of Râjpūt tribes. Vishṇu was originally an impersonation of the sun, and his *discus* (*chakra*) still recalls his ancient character. He afterwards developed into a more remote deity, and hence it is from his waking or slumbering that the destruction or reproduction of the universe occurs. Not only does Vishṇu thus give origin to all things by what may, from one point of view, be styled emanation, but he himself also becomes incarnated in various forms at different periods, in order to effect some important task. This doctrine of Vishṇu's *avatâras* or "descents" does not occur earlier than the Bhagavadgîtâ, but there we find it clearly expressed in the following lines, uttered by Vishṇu (Kṛishṇa) to Arjuna:—

> "*Yadā yadā hi dharmasya glānir bhavati, Bhārata,*
> *Abhyutthānam adharmasya, tadātmānam sṛijāmyahaṃ,*
> *Paritrāṇāya sādhūnāṃ vināśāya-ca dushkṛitāṃ.*
> *Dharma-sañsthāpanārthāya sambhavāmi yuge yuge.*"

> "For, whenever, O son of Bharata, there occurs a decrease of religion,
> An uprising of irreligion; then I produce myself.
> For the preservation of the pious and for the destruction of evil-doers,
> For the establishment of religion, I am born from age to age."[1]

Among the most famous of Vishṇu's incarnations are (1) when he became a fish to save Manu from the Flood; (2) when he became Buddha to lead astray the wicked and destroy them by inducing them to accept his false doctrines. He is also to come again as *Kalki* to destroy the *Mlechchhas* or foreigners. Many noted *gurus* or religious teachers are said to have been *avatâras* of Vishṇu, though only ten of his incarnations are generally acknowledged.

The tales of Kṛishṇa's amours with the *Gopîs* or shepherdesses are not fit to relate in English, but they are well known in India to-day, and they seem to be of perennial interest to his worshippers. There are endless legends about his birth, his warlike exploits, and, lastly, his death by a wound in the heel. His destruction and that of his people, the Yâdavas, irresistibly reminds us of the ancient Teutonic epic, the *Nibelungenlied*. One of his sons was *Kāma*, the god of sensual passion, who is sometimes identified with Kṛishṇa himself. *Rāma* is another god often invoked in India to-day, and the *Râmâyana* relates his exploits at great length. He also is a warrior, and is sometimes regarded as an *avatâra* of Vishṇu; but his moral and chivalrous character exalts him far above Kṛishṇa. His virtuous wife, *Sîtâ*, an incarnation of *Śrî* the wife of Vishṇu, was seized by *Râvaṇa*, the demon-king, and carried off to Ceylon (*Lankâ*). But Rāma, with the assistance of the monkey-king *Hanumân* (who is very widely worshipped in modern India), recovers his wife, and they become the ancestors of the ancient kings of Oudh.

Brahmâ, Śiva and Vishṇu form a triad of deities, and this dogma is supposed to represent an attempt of the Brâhmaṇs to

[1] This doctrine spread from India to other lands, for in the *Yesht-Sadeh* Ormazd is represented as informing Zoroaster that the victorious Varahrân (Bahrâm) was ten times incarnated in various forms. The Manichaeans in Europe thought Zoroaster, Buddha, Christ, and Manes one and the same, and identical with the sun. The Bābî-Bahāî sect in Persia believe that all the great prophets were one and the same person, and identify him with their founder and with the Deity. In the Egyptian "Book of the Dead" (cap. iii.) we find something not unlike the Bābî statement that the sun of to-day is the same and yet is not the same as the sun of yesterday. The Sanskṛit lines are from Bhagavadgîtâ (Bk. iv. strophes 7 and 8).

reconcile ancient Brāhmaṇism with the more popular tenets of modern Hindūism. In this system Brahmâ is the Creator, Vishṇu the Preserver, and Šiva the Destroyer. Although the sacred syllable *ôm*, which is formed by three Sanskṛit characters and represents this belief, is invested with magical effects, yet the belief in this triad does not seem at all of much importance in Hindūism. Brahmā generally plays an inferior part in comparison with Vishṇu and Šiva, and frequently seems to be forgotten altogether.

From the belief in a sexual dualism in the divine nature has sprung the hermaphrodite attributes assigned by some to Šiva. Hence came the worship of the *šakti*, the female principle, which is treated of especially in the Tantras, and has given rise to rites of a horrible and obscene nature. The *Šâkta* sect regard *Mâhâdevî* as the source of all beings, and next to her in order come many other female divinities, nearly all malignant, whose worship is generally of a horrible and revolting description. But Mahâmâyâ, "the great illusion," has two aspects of her nature, the *white* or benign, and the *black* or cruel, representing the creative or reproductive and the destructive energies respectively. To both a twofold worship is paid, that of "the right hand" in public, and that of "the left hand" in secret. The latter is of such a character that respectable Hindūs themselves are ashamed of it. Human sacrifices used to be offered to Durgâ, Kâlî, and other such female impersonations. The English Government has put a stop to this, it is believed, but not to the obscene rites connected with the *šakti*-worship.

Although we meet with profound thought and noble guesses at truth in many of both the later and the earlier sacred books of India, yet in practice the effect of Hindūism, as of every other idolatrous system, is degrading in the extreme. The devotees of Šiva outrival those of Vishṇu in such matters. "From the outset, and more than any other Hindū religion, Šivaism has pandered to ascetic fanaticism. No other has exhibited so many horrible and revolting observances, or has worn with so much ostentation the badge, often singularly enough, of devotion. . . . In our day cruel mortifications are becoming rare, yet there are still *Akâšamukhins* and *Urdhvabâhus*,—who pose themselves in immovable attitudes, their faces or their arms raised to heaven, until the sinews shrink and the posture assumed often stiffens into rigidity,—as well as *Nâgas*, *Paramahaṃsas*, *Avadhûtas*, and others, who, in spite of English interdicts, expose themselves to the inclemency of the weather in a state of absolute nudity. . . . It is not so much to merit heaven as to extort alms, by exciting terror or disgust, that the *Bahikathâs* tear their bodies with knives, and the *Aghoris* feed on carrion and excrement."[1]

Into the worship paid to Kṛishṇa and certain other gods a new element has been introduced, which is styled *bhakti* or "faith." Without this no rite or ceremony is now deemed efficacious. Hence come theories of "grace" (*anugraha*); and the abuse of these has led to the view that "a single act of faith, a single sincere invocation of the name of God, cancels a whole life of iniquity and crime. . . . In the Purâṇas it is enough, even in the case of the greatest criminal, when at the point of death, to pronounce by chance some syllables forming one of the names of Vishṇu or Šiva, in order to attain salvation."[2]

In modern times every Hindū has, or should have, a religious guide, a *guru*, whom he must in all things obey. The founders of many modern sects have thus been practically deified, and everything rests on their authority. The Mahârâjas, for instance, as the descendants of Vallabhâchârya are called, are worshipped as gods; their worshippers, male and female alike, owe them the total surrender of *tan*, *man*, *dhan*, or body, mind, and property. The licentiousness of this sect in their rites of worship is carried to an extreme, even for India.

Many reforming sects have in comparatively modern times arisen in India, some through Muḥammadan, others through Christian influences. Among the former may be mentioned the Kabîrpanthîs and the Sikhs, among the latter the Brahmo-Samâj and other more recent bodies of the same class. They all show at once the receptivity and the restlessness of the Hindū mind, and prove how utterly unable the people of India are to find the truth for themselves. At the present time Hindūism has sunk for the most part into a mixture of the most degrading idolatry, fetishism, and demonolatry. There are popularly said to be more gods in the country than men. Monkeys, cobras, and especially the cow, "the mother of the Hindūs," are devoutly adored. Each Hindū wears a tuft of hair on the top of his head as a mark of his religion, while he shaves off the rest of his hair; and the different sects are distinguished by a paint mark on the forehead. It is not neces-

[1] *The Religions of India*, pp. 214, 215.
[2] *Op. cit.* p. 228.

sary to dwell on the multitudes of idols in the temples, the almost universal use of the *linga* (phallus) as an object of worship, the great *melas* or religious festivals held at particularly holy spots, often on the banks of the sacred Ganges, the pilgrimage to Jagannāth with its terrible annual mortality, the child-marriages and the degradation of women, for all these are now well known.

Hindūism is now undoubtedly breaking down. It represents innumerable attempts to solve the great problems which the universe presents to the human soul. In India perhaps every religious theory which, apart from Revelation, has ever arisen in any other part of the world, has at some time or another been started,—often more than once, and in different forms. Starting with some comparatively true and noble conceptions of the Deity, which meet us amid the absurdities and the polytheism of the Ṛig-Veda, the Indian Âryans have gradually lost the light they once had, and wandered further and further from God. A modern Hindū scholar well exemplifies this when he says that, with all their efforts and all their philosophy, the most thoughtful and earnest minds have never, even up to the present day, been able to prove to their own satisfaction that the Deity is a Moral Being, that He loves good and hates evil. As in Greece and Rome in the past and modern Europe at the present, so also in India, every effort to find God and to know and do His will, made by the unaided intellect, has proved a failure. No merely human system has ever succeeded or will ever succeed. India needs *Christ*, and it lies with His disciples to make Him known as the Light of the World to those who in India, as we have seen, dwell in a darkness that may be felt.

CHAPTER II

BUDDHISM.

Buddhism must be regarded as one among the many attempts to reform the religion of India which have signally failed. As a philosophy, as it originally was, at once atheistic and agnostic, it has long ceased to exist. As a religious system, it has developed into several different forms of idolatry, and has spread from its original home in India to many other lands; but in India itself it can hardly be said to have any existence [1] at the present time, though it owns many adherents in Ceylon and Burma. The total number of Buddhists now in the world has been vastly exaggerated, but they possibly amount to 100,000,000.[2] The only place where Buddhism, in a very corrupt form, still lingers in India proper is in some of the valleys of Nipâl. But our treatment of the religions of India would not be complete without some account of Buddhism, not merely because the missionary has to encounter it as a formidable foe in Ceylon, but also because, absorbed again into the Hindūism from which it originally sprung, it has had a very real effect upon the latter. The limits of our subject, however, do not permit us to deal with Buddhism as it exists to-day in Tibet, China and Japan.

The most recently discovered Inscriptions of Aśoka seem to prove that Gautamo Buddha, or Siddhattho as he was originally called, died about the year B.C. 477, and was born about B.C. 557.[3] His father, Suddhodano, was a *râjâ*, and belonged to a tribe of Indo-Scythic origin, the *Śakas*, who had overrun

[1] Some Hindū sects of the present time, as the Kâṇphâṭas and the Vaishṇavavîras, show their origin by the fact that they still preserve in their calendars the names of certain Buddhist saints.

[2] Monier-Williams, *Buddhism*, pp. xv and xvii.

[3] Bühler, *Three New Edicts of Aśoka*, p. 20.

India before the Âryan invasion. They had, however, in all probability intermarried with the Âryans, as the family belonged to the Kshatriya caste. Buddha's mother, Mâyâ, is said to have died very shortly after her son's birth; but he was brought up by a sister of hers, Mahâpajâpati, another of his father's wives. The Sanskṛit biographies of Buddha which we have were composed many centuries after his death, and are full of the most marvellous legends. The Pālî canonical books contain no biography of him, unless we dignify with that name a short poem in the *Buddhavaṃsa*,[1] though we have an account of his last few months and of his death.[2] The received Pālî works, though ancient, are of uncertain date and authorship, and are composed in a dialect considerably different from and probably more recent than that contained in Aśoka's inscriptions, written more than 250 years after Gautamo's death. He was married to one or more wives, probably about the age of 16 or 17 years. At the age of 29, having already learnt that earthly joys do not bring happiness, he left his home and became an ascetic, joining himself to one after another famous teacher of his time. Failing to find rest in asceticism, he developed a system of his own, which he taught to his disciples. The latter he sent forth to preach his Law. He continued to teach until his death in extreme old age.

His philosophy was the natural outcome of his time, and contains very little if anything new. Yet its discovery so delighted him that from that time he designated himself the "Buddha" (the *Knower*), and deemed himself superior to all the gods of India. His lofty claims are thus stated in his own words:—

"I have overcome all foes; I am all-wise; I am free from stains in every way; I have left everything; and I have obtained emancipation by the destruction of desire. Having myself gained knowledge, whom should I call my master? I have no teacher; no one is equal to me; in the world of men and of gods no being is like me. I am the Holy One in this world, I am the highest teacher, I alone am the absolute Sambuddho; I have gained coolness (by the extinction of all passion), and have obtained *Nirvâṇa*. To found the Kingdom of the Law I go to the city of the Kâśîs (Banâras); I will beat the drum of the Immortal in the darkness of this world." He goes on to boast of having overcome all states of sinfulness.

[1] Chap. xxvi. [2] In the Mahâparinibbâna-Suttaṃ.

In such a system as this there was no room for a God. Buddhism therefore knew of no Creator and no Judge of the world: his system was from the beginning atheistic in the sense of not even seeking to attain to any knowledge of the Divine, though he admitted the existence of spirits innumerable of different classes, and that of many heavens and hells. But none of these spirits, however high their rank, were, he held, entitled to worship, being all inferior to Buddha himself, though he confessed himself a mere man.

The whole of the main doctrines of Buddhism, as it originally was, are briefly summed up in the first of the many discourses which Buddha is said to have delivered. As handed down by tradition, his speech ran thus:—

"There[1] are two extremes, O Mendicants, which he who has given up the world ought to avoid. A life given up to pleasures, devoted to pleasures and lusts: this is degrading, sensual, vulgar, ignoble, profitless; and a life given over to mortifications: this is painful, ignoble, and profitless. By avoiding these two extremes, O Mendicants, the "Perfected One" (*Tathâgato*, one of Buddha's titles) "has gained the knowledge of the Middle Path, which leads to insight, which leads to wisdom, which conduces to calm, to knowledge, to the Perfect Buddhahood, to extinction" (*Nirvâṇa*, Pāli *Nibbânam*).

"Which, O Mendicants, is this Middle Path, the knowledge of which the Perfected One has gained, which leads to insight, . . . to extinction? It is the Noble Eightfold Path, namely, Perfect Opinion, perfect resolve, perfect speech, perfect employment, perfect conduct, perfect exertion, perfect thought, perfect self-concentration. This, O Mendicants, is the Middle Path, the knowledge of which the Perfected One has gained, which leads . . . to extinction.

"This, O Mendicants, is the Noble Truth of *Suffering*. Birth is suffering, decay is suffering, illness is suffering, death is suffering, presence of hated objects is suffering, separation from loved objects is suffering, not to obtain what is desired is suffering. Briefly, the fivefold clinging to existence is suffering."

Buddha then goes on to explain the cause of this universal suffering. It is produced, he says, by Thirst, which is of three kinds: thirst for sensual pleasure, for future existence and for the cessation of existence. The way to escape from suffering, therefore, is to put an end to all such desires. This is to be

[1] Dhamma-cakkapp-avattana-Suttam.

done only by pursuing the Noble Eightfold Path, the several stages in which have been already mentioned.

According to this address we see that the "Gospel of Buddha," as it has in recent times been called, consisted in teaching men that all existence is misery, and that the only possible way of escape from misery and suffering lies in ceasing to exist. Not only men, but the *devas* and all other superhuman beings, and all the rest of the inhabitants of the universe, whether in one of the 26 heavens or in the 136 hells, are all alike bound together in this endless chain of suffering. All alike are interested in Buddha's great discovery, for only by pursuing the "Noble Eightfold Path" can any being attain to the cessation of suffering. To accomplish this one single aim all effort should be directed. Hence it was that Buddha directly discouraged all inquiry into such matters as the origin of the universe, the existence of God, and every other one of those deep and most serious questions which have in all ages seemed to most earnest and thoughtful men to be of the very first importance. He denounced "Ignorance" indeed, as the cause of all evil, but by *ignorance* he meant only ignorance of the "Four Noble Truths" which he had discovered. All other knowledge than this, he held, was worthless,—a hindrance rather than a help. By attaining this knowledge Buddha believed himself to have become superior to all the gods. They therefore became his humble and devoted disciples; for Brahmâ himself, we are told, did not venture to address him except kneeling and with the greatest reverence and humility.

Buddha did not believe in the immortality of the soul. In fact he distinctly taught that man has no spirit, no personality, no *Ego*. Man is a compound, made up of various constituent parts, which are separated at death. The human being therefore at death ceases to exist. But death does not suffice to deliver him from suffering; for, unless he has been able entirely to work out and exhaust his *Karma*, he will be born again in some other state of existence, perhaps as an animal, possibly as an evil spirit, or again as one of the *devas*. The doctrine of transmigration was so universally received in India in Buddha's time (though it seems to have formed no part of the original creed of the Âryans) that he accepted it without question. Yet at the same time it required modification to prevent it from coming in conflict with the denial of the existence of a spirit in man. The doctrine, thus modified, may be stated thus. When any living being dies, at that very moment another being starts into existence, most intimately connected with the former; and to the new being all the "fruit" of the deeds, good and bad, done by the former, is transferred. Every evil deed must thus be expiated by suffering, while every good deed brings its own reward. To explain this passing on of existence, the simile of the candle or torch was employed. If a number of candles, or, better still, pieces of tinder, are placed in close proximity to one another, and the first lighted, then the breath which extinguishes it will kindle the next, and so on. The second flame is not the same as the first, though produced from it. So at the death of one being, another starts into existence. It was so difficult, however, to express the connection with one another of such distinct yet related beings, that Buddha often uses exactly the popular language, which expressed belief in transmigration. Thus he tells how, before his last and final birth, he had himself existed in a vast number of previous states,—as an elephant, as a monkey, as Prince Vessantaro, and so on. There is therefore not much practical difference between the Buddhist and the Hindū doctrine of transmigration.

Now the whole object of Buddha's teaching was to enable his followers to attain to extinction of being by their own unaided exertions. All existence is misery, therefore in order to be free from misery, it is necessary to cease to exist.

But existence is caused by *thirst*, therefore the Buddhist must strive to overcome that which causes that thirst. He must endeavour, by walking in the Noble Eightfold Path, to become indifferent to all things, good and bad, earthly and heavenly alike. When he has thus burst all "bonds," he has attained Nirvâṇa even in this life, and when he dies he will not be reborn. Nirvâṇa is often used of such a final death, but its strict sense is the "extinction" of passion, from which proceeds in turn the extinction of being.

The Community (*Saṅgho*) which Buddha founded was a community of mendicants, clad in yellow robes, and obliged to beg their bread from door to door.[1] These were at first exclusively *men*, but Buddha ultimately, at Mahâpajâpati's earnest request, suffered women to join it. There were many "lay adherents," drawn generally from the higher castes and the wealthy portion of society, but these were not members of

[1] *Buddha*, Eng. trans. pp. 156–158.

the Community. Their main duty was to provide for the wants of the monks and nuns, which they did most liberally, bestowing on the *Saṅgho* lands in the neighbourhood of cities, especially at Kapalavastu, Vesâlî, and Uruvelâ. Buddha and his disciples though professing (like all other Mendicant Orders of the time) to admit to their ranks men of every caste and nationality, yet practically addressed themselves mostly to the very highest, or at least obtained most of their converts and adherents from them. King Bimbisâro of Magadha and Pasenadi of Kosala (Oudh and Bihâr) were among his chief patrons. Professor Oldenberg remarks that he is "not aware of any instance in which a Chaṇḍâlo—the pariah of that age—is mentioned in the sacred writings as a member of the Order. For the lower order of the people, for those born to toil in manual labour, hardened by the struggle for existence, the announcement of the connexion of misery with all forms of existence was not made, nor was the dialectic of the law of the painful concatenation of causes and effects calculated to satisfy the 'poor in spirit.' 'To the wise belongeth this law,' it is said, 'not to the foolish.' Very unlike the word of that Man who suffered 'little children to come unto' Him, 'for of such is the Kingdom of God.' For children, and those who are like children, the arms of Buddha are not open." And again, "Princes[1] and nobles, Brâhmaṇs and merchants, we find among those who 'took their refuge in Buddha, the Law and the Order,' *i.e.* who made their profession as lay believers. The wealthy and the aristocrat, it seems, here also exceeded the poor. To reach the humble and wretched, the sorrowing, who endured yet another sorrow than the great, universal sorrow of impermanence, was not the province of Buddhism."

In this respect we perceive how distinctly Buddhism proved itself to be, not a religion but a philosophy. Like all philosophies of Europe and Asia, of ancient and modern times alike, Buddhism addresses itself to the chosen few, the cultured and wealthy. It has no message of comfort and encouragement for the poor, the outcast, the sick, the oppressed, the guilty but penitent transgressor. Not "to the poor" but to the rich was proclaimed the Law of the Middle Path. Certain entire classes of people were, for various reasons, refused leave to enter the Community.[2] Buddhism was no better adapted, even *in its original and*

[1] *Op. cit.* p. 163.

[2] Mahâvaggo, I. caps. xxxix., xl., xliv., xlv., xlvi., xlvii. etc. etc.

uncorrupt form, to universal acceptance than were the somewhat similar theoretical philosophies of the Epicureans and Stoics in later times. We are not, therefore, surprised to find kings like Pasenadi and Bimbisâro among Buddha's lay admirers, any more than to discover the Emperor Aurelius Antoninus among the professors of the philosophy of the Porch. And if we find among the adherents of Zeno's school a slave like Epictetus, or among Buddha's disciples a man of humble position like Thero Sunîto, the exception merely proves the truth of the general rule.

Buddha had no doubt a considerable amount of opposition to encounter, but it arose more from the natural grief felt by parents and relatives at seeing their children and connexions renounce the world to become monks than from anything else. His teaching in this respect, however, was in accordance with what had long been universally taught and held in India as necessary for deliverance from the bondage of the flesh. It differed, in fact, from the teaching of the Jains and other sects principally in condemning the extreme asceticism and self-torture which the members of such sects in India then inflicted and still continue to inflict on themselves. Instead of being opposed to and by the Brâhmaṇs, as is generally asserted, Buddha reckoned considerable numbers of them among his disciples and adherents, and he very frequently used the word *Brâhmaṇ* to denote the very highest and most earnest of his own followers. Moreover, the influence of the Brâhmaṇs in the North-Eastern part of India, in which alone Buddha passed his life, was far less pronounced at that time than in the Western. He doubtless found the rivalry of other monkish and ascetic communities a more serious hindrance, but he had no persecution to fear, no danger to shun.

Buddha died at Kusinârâ at the age of eighty. In his last discourses he said to his disciples that they should "abide as their own Refuge, recognising no other refuge, having the Law as their lamp, having the Law as their refuge, recognising no other refuge."[1] His last recorded words were these: "Come now, Mendicants, I bid you farewell. Compounds are subject to decay. Prosper ye through diligence."[2]

The whole of the orthodox Buddhist doctrines rest upon the authority of Buddha himself. He claimed no inspiration, but

[1] Mahâparinibbâna-Suttam, pp. 22, 23, ed. Childers.
[2] *Op. cit.* p. 61.

declared that he had obtained omniscience and the recollection of all that had ever happened to himself in earlier births. Our knowledge of his teaching is derived from the sacred Pālī books of the *Tipiṭakam*, the most ancient portions of which Professor Rhys Davids thinks were composed about 150 years after Buddha's death.[1] But the fact that the language in which they are written is different from, and apparently more *recent* than, the Magadhî, in which Aśoka's edicts were composed some 250 years after Buddha's *Nirvâṇa*,[2] renders their great antiquity somewhat doubtful. The Sanskṛit Buddhist literature of Nipâl is very much later and altogether devoid of authority, being a mere mass of the most absurd fables. It is, however, useful in enabling us to understand the process of the gradual corruption of Buddhism, until it reached the form which it has now assumed.

So much has been written in praise of Buddha's ethical system that it behoves us to examine it, though necessarily very briefly. Buddha doubtless uttered many noble sentiments and denounced immorality, but his moral system is nevertheless very imperfect from the fact that, caring to know nothing of God, he naturally looked at everything from a utilitarian or essentially selfish standpoint. The Buddhist cannot acknowledge that he owes any duty to the God in whom he does not believe. Only to his fellow-beings, men and the lower animals, does he owe any duty at all. As, moreover, the only thing about which he has to concern himself is to free himself from the fetters of existence, all his moral ideas are conditioned by the desire to attain this goal as speedily as possible. Good and evil have no strictly moral significance, in fact have no real existence. They are said by modern Buddhists to differ merely in degree and not in kind. While, therefore, there is much that is good and noble in Buddha's precepts, there is also not a little that is defective and even wrong. Those duties which are incumbent upon the Buddhist are so because, and only because, their performance is supposed to aid him in ultimately attaining *Nirvâṇa*. Other things are forbidden because they tend to evil consequences, by hindering him from so speedily reaching that wretched goal. The foundation of the whole of Buddhist morality is therefore found in the Four Noble Truths already stated. Professor Rhys Davids well says that the

[1] *Hibbert Lectures*, 1881, p. 43.
[2] Bühler, *Three New Edicts of Aśoka*.

moral system of genuine Buddhism consisted of three great divisions. "There was a system of lower morality intended for those who wished to remain in the world. There was a second system, including the lower but going beyond it, for those who had entered the Order. And there was a third and highest, including both the others, but going again beyond them, for those who had entered the Noble Eightfold Path,—that is to say, the system of intellectual and moral self-culture and self-control which culminated in *Arahat*-ship. What we understand by morality is almost confined to the *lowest* of the three." [1]

The Ten "Moral Precepts" of the Buddhist faith are divided into three sections. The first five of these precepts are binding upon lay adherents, who are not obliged to obey the remainder, but they are recommended to observe the first eight. All members of the Order, and all novices and catechumens, are pledged to keep all ten. These precepts [2] enjoin—

(1) Abstinence from slaying any living being.
(2) Abstinence from taking what is not given.
(3) Abstinence from conduct unbecoming a religious student.
(4) Abstinence from speaking falsely.
(5) Abstinence from intoxicants, which cause slothfulness.

(6) Abstinence from eating out of due season.
(7) Abstinence from dancing, songs, music, and seeing spectacles.
(8) Abstinence from using as adornments garlands, scents, unguents, ornaments, and finery.

(9) Abstinence from (sleeping in) a high bed, a big bed.
(10) Abstinence from receiving gold and silver.

The Third Moral Precept is held to forbid all kinds of unchastity, while a member of the Order has to live as a celibate. But the *Mahâvaggo* speaks of bestiality as far less wicked than the conduct of a mendicant who returns to his family,[3] thus showing how terribly perverted the moral sense becomes in a faith which does not recognise a God. The First Precept forbids taking the life even of an animal, the reason being that all beings are bound together by transmigration.

[1] *Hibbert Lectures* for 1881, pp. 205, 206.
[2] Mahâvaggo, I. lvi.
[3] Mahâvaggo, I. lxxviii. § 2.

Thus the guilt of murder and the innocent act of killing an animal for food or putting to death a noxious reptile are classed together, even though in practice a difference is recognised between them.

The idea of "Sin" is necessarily absent from Buddha's ethical system, which in its stead recognises only *defilement* (*âsavo*) and *passion* (*kileso*).

Nearly all the Buddhist precepts are *negative* in their character, requiring abstinence from certain conduct rather than active well-doing. It has been held that the direction to practise universal benevolence in the *Metta-suttam* is an exception to this. Yet this precept also is urged on the plea that such conduct benefits the *doer*, and tends to enable him to reach Nirvâṇa. But it is somewhat difficult to discover precisely what is implied by this "benevolence," which is not to be confounded with *beneficence*. Buddhism does not enjoin upon its devotees the duty of comforting the sorrowful, helping the poor, healing the sick, or even performing ordinary duties towards parents or children, except in the case of lay adherents, and these are not properly members of the Order. The further one advances along the "Noble Eightfold Path," the less is expected. The monk has abandoned his family, as Buddha himself did, and he is warned against feeling affection towards any human being, as this would bind him to existence and hinder his attainment of Nirvâṇa as effectually as yielding to sensuality would do. Hence it is that in the *Dhammapadaṃ* Buddha defines the perfect man as "he who has overcome both good and evil, both bonds,"[1] and says that he should avoid loving anyone as well as hating anyone.[2]

Buddhism is a creed of pessimism, it sees no purpose in life, no hope in death; the one thing it aims at is extinction. It sees no dignity in labour, nothing that is not degrading, or at least enslaving, in the noblest human affections: its highest human ideal is an idle mendicant, "bound by no ties, human or divine." Hence Buddhism ultimately failed and died out even in the land of its birth. In other lands, corrupted into a system of idolatry, it still lingers on, despised through the vices to which idleness has given birth among its mendicants, and unable to effect[3] any moral reformation even by its good

[1] Dhammapadaṃ, Śloka 412. [2] *Op. cit.* Śll. 210–215.

[3] In the "Circular in connection with the Chinese Emergency," issued by the Buddhists of Japan, and dated 11th October 1900, the theory is

precepts, because it appeals and can appeal to no noble and unselfish motive in the hearts and consciences of men.

In Ceylon[1] at the present time Buddhism has no very high moral standard. Many of the monks live impure lives. They often teach the young, but do little in the way of preaching. They have little influence on the laity. The latter are very much more under the influence of the demon-priests; and practically demonolatry, coupled with occasional pilgrimages to *dagobas*,—shrines where some supposed relics of Buddha are preserved and almost worshipped,—constitutes their religion. A revival of a purer Buddhism, distinguished principally for its attacks on Christianity, has, during the last twenty years, taken place in Colombo, principally through European influence, and it has spread to certain other parts of the country. Buddhism is not, even by its professors in Ceylon, supposed to have much to do with daily life. The very name of the "Noble Eightfold Path" is hardly known, except among those who have come under European influence. No one attempts to walk in it, nor does anyone hope in this life to become an *arahat*, and attain to Nirvâṇa at death. There are four different sects of monks, but they differ little from one another. The lower caste people are not admitted to the Community. Only a portion of the inhabitants make any profession of Buddhism at all: most of the remainder are Hindūs. The most earnest revivalists among the Ceylon Buddhists absolutely deny the existence of God. From such a system what hope, for time or for eternity, can be derived?

tacitly accepted that the Buddhists in China have been at the bottom of the whole Boxer movement. The Japanese Buddhists say that they have "perceived, with no small regret, that Buddhism in China has so completely declined as to have lost all vestige of influence upon the morals of men" (*vide C.M.S. Intelligencer* for February 1901, p. 118).

[1] See Bishop Copleston's account, *Buddhism*, p. 415 sqq.

CHAPTER III

MUḤAMMADANISM.

The "Religion of Islâm," as it is called by those who profess it, owes its spread in India in times past entirely to the sword. It was introduced by the Mughul conquerors from Persia and Afghânistân, and forcibly imposed upon many of the conquered race. Their descendants and the descendants of their conquerors, together with a certain number who have been won over to Islâm in more recent times by various secular inducements, constitute, for the most part, the 60 million Muslims of India. There are also a few Arabs and Persians who have for various reasons settled in Bombay, Calcutta, and other seaport towns. It cannot be said that at the present day in India the Muḥammadans are superior or even equal to the Hindūs in morality, industry, or culture. In fact the Government of India find it necessary to show special encouragement to Muḥammadan youths, in order to prevent the Hindūs from filling almost every post of importance under Government.[1] But their number and their fanaticism for their religion render the Muḥammadans an important factor in the population of the country. In some places, more especially in the Panjāb, much work has been done among them, and many converts won of all classes, from the highest to the lowest. Among the best known of the former may be mentioned Dr. 'Imâdu'd Dîn, Dr. Barkhurdâr Khân, 'Abdu'llâh Athîm, Ṣafdar 'Alî, Iḥsânu'llâh, Jânî 'Alî, and many others, some of whom have passed away. Dr. 'Imâdu'd Dîn, in a paper read at the Chicago "Parliament of Religions," gives the names and short biographies of 117 such leading men, who were once Muslims but were converted to Christianity.

[1] Many posts are now filled by Indian Christians, who are coming to the fore in learning and in every other way.

As is well known, the founder of Islâm was Muḥammad, an Arab of the Quraish tribe, who was born at Mecca in the year 570 of the Christian era. The main facts of his life have become well known to the English reader, mainly through his biography, written by Sir William Muir from Arabic sources. He was forty-two years of age when he first, in A.D. 612, laid claim to the prophetic office. His wife, Khadîjah, and some of his near relatives were his first converts; and his followers underwent so much persecution that many of them ultimately fled to Abyssinia, to the court of the Christian king who reigned there. After a short time, however, just before Muḥammad's own departure (*Hijrah*) from Mecca in A.D. 622, many of them returned, and accompanied him to Medînah, where the majority of the people made an alliance with him against their hereditary foes in Mecca. Muḥammad first enriched his followers with the plunder of three neighbouring Jewish tribes, and then began to despoil the Meccan caravans. Eight years after the Hijrah, in A.D. 630, Muḥammad was able to make himself master of Mecca and the Ka'bah, the great ancestral temple of the Arabs there. Established and spread by the irresistible logic of the sword, the new religion soon dominated Arabia. All opponents were slain or banished; and when Muḥammad died in A.D. 632, he had become ruler of the whole country, and was about to lead his armies to the conquest of Syria and Persia. His successors, the Khalîfehs, continued the same martial conduct, and their success in overrunning both those countries and many others is too well known to need repeating here.

Regarding the religion taught by Muḥammad, it may be briefly described as a Jewish heresy mixed with ideas derived from apocryphal Christian books and even from Zoroastrian and other Eastern sources, among which many of the tenets and practices of the heathen Arabs hold by no means the least important place. Its creed is well described by Gibbon as consisting of an eternal truth and a necessary fiction—"There is no god but God; Muḥammad is the Apostle of God." Muḥammad taught certain great truths, and these constitute the strength of Islâm to the present day. The most important of these are—(1) The Unity of God and His Almighty Power, Omnipresence, and Omniscience. (2) Man's dependence upon his Creator, his need of prayer and of the Prophets and inspired books, which God has sent him by their hands. (3) The certainty of an After-life, in which the just are rewarded and the wicked punished. But Muḥammad is regarded as the last and greatest of all the Prophets; and the Qur'ân, revealed to him through the Archangel Gabriel, has annulled all previous revelations, more especially the New Testament. Muḥammad is related by tradition to have summed up the chief doctrines and precepts of his religion in these words: "Islâm is founded upon five matters: (1) the testifying that there is no god but God, and that Muḥammad is His Servant and His Apostle; (2) the offering of the stated Prayers; (3) the payment of *zakât* (alms enjoined by the Divine law); (4) the Pilgrimage to Mecca; and (5) fasting during Ramazân.

Muḥammad's teaching,[1] even with reference to the three great truths previously mentioned, is not free from very grave defects. It is the glory of Islâm that it teaches that God alone should be worshipped, that it recognises God as Personal, Omniscient and Almighty, the Creator and Preserver, the Master and Judge of all Creation. But of a God of infinite Holiness, of infinite Justice and of infinite Love, Muḥammad had absolutely no conception. Among the 99 Most Excellent Names of God which the Muslims repeat and sometimes engrave on their tombs, the title of *Father* does not occur. Not only so, but Muḥammadans think that to use such a word to express God's relationship to His creatures is to blaspheme. Their theologians assure us that the gulf between the Divine and the human is so immeasurable that no inferences with regard to God's dealings with us can possibly be drawn from considering what our intuitions with reference to justice or holiness teach us. Thus Al Ghazzālī says of God, "Nor is His justice to be compared with the justice of men, because a man may be suspected of acting unjustly by invading the possession of another; but no injustice can be conceived of God, who can find nothing belonging to any other besides Himself." Captain Osborn well writes: "There is no creed the inner life of which has been so completely crushed under an inexorable weight of ritual. For that deep, impassable gulf which divides man from God empties all religious acts of spiritual life and meaning, and reduces them to rites and ceremonies." A German author, writing on the subject, says that,

[1] For authorities see my *Religion of the Crescent*, and in a shorter form, my paper on "Islâm: its Origin, its Strength, and its Weakness," read before the Victoria Institute on December 7, 1891.

however much Muḥammad "discourses about God's Righteousness, His Wrath against Sin, His Grace and Mercy, yet Allâh is not holy love, not the negation of all self-seeking and sensuality. Neither in holiness nor in love is He just. Towards the ungodly, love does not attain to its right. Allâh is quick and ready enough to punish them, to lead them astray, and to harden their hearts: His wrath is not free from passion. Towards believers, that holiness which can love nothing impure is wanting. Allâh can permit His Prophet to do things that would elsewhere be objectionable: to the rest of believers, too, He can permit what is not of itself good. . . . The commandments which Allâh gives are not the expression of His Nature; they are arbitrary, and can therefore be retracted and replaced by others. Thus the God of Muḥammad leaves upon us the impression of an arbitrary Oriental despot, who makes His enemies experience His wrath in a terrible manner, and loads His faithful servants with benefits, besides winking at their misdeeds."

The one attribute of God which to the Muslim mind towers above and almost overshadows all others, is His almighty *Power*. Islâm may with good reason be styled the deification of Power. This power may be exercised in the most arbitrary manner, and is unrestrained by any Law of Holiness or Justice inherent in God's very Being. Hence it is that Muslims fail to see the moral obliquity of many of their Prophet's actions. "If *we* were to do such a thing, it would be murder, or adultery, as the case may be," they say; "but when Muḥammad, the chosen, the Apostle of God, acted thus, he committed no sin, for God *permitted him to do so as a sign of His favour unto him.*" The fact that it is a moral impossibility for God to sanction, much less to enjoin, the commission of distinct breaches of the eternal Moral Law, is quite beyond their comprehension; and the enunciation of the statement that God *could* not reward His Prophet by granting him permission to break that law without incurring guilt and deserving punishment, appears to Muḥammad's followers to be a blasphemous denial of the Omnipotence of the Deity.

One of the leading features in the Religion of Muḥammad is the belief it inculcates in an inexorable Fate, by which all things in heaven and on earth are bound for time and for eternity. Tradition informs us that, before He created the world, God caused to be written down on the Preserved Tablet all that should happen on earth, even to the extent of the movement of the leaf of a tree in the breeze. The eternal happiness or misery of a man in the next world, as well as his every action here, was, they tell us, determined upon in the Divine decree long before that man was created. The Qur'ân represents God as saying, "Verily I will fill Hell with men and genii,"[1] and makes Him declare that He had created them for that very purpose.[2] "God," we are assured, "misleadeth whom He willeth, and guideth aright whom He willeth,"[3] and He says of Himself in the Qur'ân,[4] "As for every man, We have firmly fixed his fate" (literally, *his bird*) "upon his neck." It is needless to dwell longer upon this matter as it is so generally known; but the bad effect of such a system of fatalism is incalculable.

The word *Islâm* properly denotes *resignation* or *self-surrender*, but it is to such a deity as this—the resignation which springs from impotence, terror and despair. The proper and most fitting attitude of the pious Muslim towards God, as Muḥammadan writers tell us, is that of a corpse in the hands of the washers of the dead.

Although the obligation to offer prayer to God is most fully recognised by every Muslim, yet Islâm fails to realise what prayer should be. It is regarded as a duty imposed upon us by the arbitrary *fiat* of God, rather than as a spiritual means of refreshment and as enabling the worshipper to hold communion in spirit with God. Of such communion, indeed, Muḥammad never even dreamed. It is one of the attractions of Paradise to a Muslim that there, he believes, as he will be freed from all other burdens, so too he will be released from all necessity of worshipping God. The worshipper is by the religious laws of Islâm required, while here below, to offer homage to his Lord at five fixed times in the day, and in doing so he must use definitely prescribed genuflexions and prostrations, and he is obliged to conform to the appointed ritual with the greatest precision. If he fails in this his prayer is rendered ineffectual, nay rather it is turned into sin, and no amount of heart devotion can render it acceptable to God. "Resting on the arms while at prayer is pleasing to the people of Hell," said Muḥammad. The amount of merit attached to prayer is very greatly dependent upon the place where it is offered. "A

[1] Sûrahs xi. 120 and xxxii. 13.
[2] Sûrahs xi. 120 and vii. 178.
[3] Sûrah lxxiv. 34.
[4] Sûrah xvii. 14.

6

prayer in this mosque of mine," he said at Medîna on another occasion, "is better than a thousand prayers anywhere else, except at the Holy Mosque" at Mecca. At another time he said, "A man's prayer in the congregation exceeds in value twenty-five times his prayer in his own house." Public prayers must always be in Arabic, even though the great mass of the worshippers may be utterly unable to comprehend the words they utter. Even when offered privately, the prescribed prayers must be in Arabic; though, when he has offered these, the worshipper may then, if he pleases, address God in his own language.

The account which Qatâdah gives of Muḥammad's "Night Journey" to Heaven shows clearly how defective the Muḥammadan conception of prayer is. We are informed that on that occasion God commanded Muḥammad to bid his followers to offer the stated prayers fifty times a day. By Moses' advice, however, Muḥammad requested some relief from this intolerable "burden," and at last the number was reduced to five. Then a celestial herald proclaimed in God's name, "I have completed My injunction and removed a *burden* from My servants."

The directions given by Muḥammad regarding prayer are very formal if rather puerile. "When any one of you says his prayers, he *must* have something in front of him; but if he cannot find anything else for that purpose, he must stick his staff into the ground. But if the ground be hard, then let him place it lengthways before him. But if he has no staff, he must draw a line on the ground, after which there will be no detriment to his prayers from anyone passing in front of it." Previous to prayer the hands and feet must be washed in water, or, if there be no water obtainable, then the same form must be gone through with sand. When one day Muḥammad and a party of followers were lying in wait for a caravan which they wished to plunder, the time of prayer was announced. Just as they had begun to prepare for their devotions, the caravan appeared. Some of them, therefore, in hastening their ablutions in order to begin the pious work of attacking and plundering their enemies, instead of dipping their feet into the water, merely poured the water over them as they stood on the desert sands. The soles of their feet therefore remained dry when they performed their devotions. When Muḥammad heard of this he said, "Woe to the soles of their feet, for they shall be in hell fire!" In order to worship correctly, the safest thing is to imitate Muḥammad as exactly as possible, because the Angel Gabriel instructed him what postures to adopt during prayer. In reality Muḥammad imitated the Jews of his time in at least certain respects, believing that, as they were the "People of the Book" and children of Abraham, their method of worship must be right. Hence the resemblance which Muslims themselves notice between their habit of praying in public places, at the corners of the street and in the market-places, and that of the Pharisees of our Lord's day, whose conduct in this respect was so sternly reproved by Him on the ground of hypocrisy. Prayer and ceremonial rites, when performed in such a way, have no good effect upon the heart and conscience. The exaltation of the outer ceremonial over the inner kernel of adoration must tend to deaden all aspirations after a more spiritual worship. Thus, in reference to prayer as well as to almost everything else, Islâm gives man a stone when he asks for the bread of life.

The shallowness of the Muḥammadan conception of Sin is one of the weakest of the many weak points in Islâm, affecting as it does the whole of human conduct, the whole system of morality, both theoretical and practical, and even the very idea of the Divine nature. A Muslim would define sin as merely the transgression of an arbitrary decree of the Deity, which decree He may rescind at His pleasure. Thus many actions which are sinful, because prohibited, here, will be perfectly innocent in the next world. For example, there are clear indications in the Qur'ân that Muḥammad regarded a *very* great excess of unchastity on earth as a sin. Yet the reason for this was, he no doubt held, merely the fact that God had prohibited it. In itself there could not have been very much in such conduct contrary to the mind of God, else Muḥammad would not have obtained special permission to indulge in greater sensuality than even other believers; this particular privilege being given to him as a sign of God's favour towards His chosen Apostle. Moreover, if a Muḥammadan here restrains himself within the very wide limits afforded him by sanctioned polygamy, almost unlimited permission to divorce and remarry, and the servile concubinage directly and expressly approved of in the Qur'ân, then, as a reward for his obedience to God's law, he will be permitted to indulge to the full in the most shameless licentiousness in Paradise before the very throne of God Himself.

It is clear how much such ideas detract from any conception of God's holiness. The title of "Holy" is given to God by the Muḥammadans, who doubtless learnt it from the Jews, but it is evident that the deity whom they conceive of is not holy. It is not possible, therefore, for Islâm to inculcate holiness and pureness of heart and life. The basis upon which Muḥammadan morality rests is *fear* and *selfishness*, hence there can be no hope that it will ever develop into anything very lofty, pure and self-denying. Man's *fallen* nature is practically regarded as his true and original one. He is therefore essentially sensual, and will for ever require sensual gratifications in order to be truly happy.

Sin is, moreover, regarded either as a disease to be cured by almsgiving, pilgrimages etc., or as an outward defilement which may be washed away by the recitation of the stated prayers. On one occasion it is related that Muḥammad inquired of some of his followers, "If there be a river at the gate of any one of you, in which he bathes five times a day, will there remain any defilement upon him?" When they replied in the negative, Muḥammad said, "Then that is what the Five Prayers are like; by means of them God wipes out sins."

There is in Islâm no Atonement, nay the idea of the very possibility of such is repugnant to the Qur'ân. Yet among the Shî'ahs of Persia and those of the same sect in India, a belief has arisen that perhaps the deaths of Ḥasan and Ḥusain, the Prophet's grandsons, may be regarded as an atonement for the sins of those who put their trust in them. Denying—as Muḥammadans do deny—the death of Jesus Christ upon the Cross, and entirely rejecting the doctrine that He was anything more than a great Prophet, whose dispensation came to an end when Muḥammad appeared, Muslims naturally deny our Lord's Atonement. Hence, feeling the insufficiency of their good deeds and their prayers to deliver them from the punishment due to them for their sins, some of the most earnest Muslims have lived and died in the greatest misery. Of Abû 'Imrân, a celebrated Imâm, it is related that, when he knew he must soon die, he was greatly distressed in mind. Asked the reason of this he replied, "What peril can be greater than mine? I must expect a messenger from my Lord, sent to announce to me either Paradise or Hell. I declare solemnly I would rather remain as I am now, with my soul struggling in my throat till the Resurrection Day, than undergo such a hazard."

Bishop Boyd Carpenter has well said that true religion makes provision for three things in Man's relation to his Maker—for dependence upon God, for fellowship with God, and for progress in the knowledge of God and of His works. Islâm provides for one of these, and for one only. Man is dependent upon God, Muḥammad teaches, but as a slave and not as a son. He can know nothing of God but what has been revealed in a book—the Qur'ân. Between Man and God there is absolutely no resemblance. The only way to approach God is by reciting the prayers which He has enjoined, in the manner prescribed through Muḥammad. Progress in morality or in anything else is unnecessary, perhaps impossible, certainly impious. The laws drawn up for Arabs in the seventh century of the Christian era, representing as they do many of their time-honoured practices, are stereotyped for all ages of the world's history, and for all lands and races alike. They are God's laws; and to change them, or even to conceive the wish to do so, would be a proof of infidelity. Slavery, polygamy, the veil and all the degradation that these things imply and produce, are, according to the Muḥammadan, parts of God's law, Divinely sanctioned institutions which must endure unto the end of the world. Even Christ, who ascended up to heaven without dying, they say, when He comes again, will compel all men to accept Islâm ere He dies and is interred in the empty tomb which now awaits him between the graves of Muḥammad and Abû Bakr at Medînah.

As much that is erroneous has been written regarding the attitude of Muḥammadans towards the Bible, it may be well to explain very briefly what that attitude is. The Qur'ân itself, in 131 different places, refers to the Old and New Testaments, though only once directly and once indirectly quoting them, and on every such occasion speaks of them as of Divine origin. But, through wresting a few verses (in which the Jews are accused by Muḥammad of "twisting their tongues" and otherwise trying to deceive him as to the teachings of the Old Testament), Muḥammadans at the present day fancy that they can prove from the Qur'ân that our Scriptures have been corrupted. In India some are learned enough to see the force of the Christian argument, that the Bible in Muḥammad's day was just as it is now, but in other lands this is not yet admitted by any Muslims. The opinion that Christ at His Ascension took the New Testament away with Him into heaven is still prevalent in many places. Unless where they have been prevailed upon to read the Bible, Muḥammadans have the most confused and legendary beliefs about the Prophets. They say that there were 124,000 of them, some being greater than others. Muslims are in the Qur'ân bidden to profess belief in all the Prophets and in the books revealed to them, regarding the number of which opinions vary. But they all hold that they need study no religious books except the Qur'ân and the Traditions of Muḥammad. It was this belief that led the Khalîfeh 'Umar to burn the Alexandrian Library, as Abû'l Faraj informs us, and to order Ṣa'd, the conqueror of Persia, to destroy the libraries which he found in that country, as the writer of the Kashfu'ẓ Ẕunūn states.

The devotion to Science and Literature, which was so noticeable in Baghdâd and at Cordova in the times of the Khalîfehs of the House of 'Abbâs, is no longer found in India or in any other land among, at least, the great mass of Muḥammadans of the present day.[1] The reason of this is not far to seek. That movement was contrary to the spirit of Islâm, and was due to the then prevalence of a party called the *Mu'tazilah* or Rationalists, who had practically rejected Muḥammadanism. It soon lost its influence, and has never recovered it.

The attitude of Muḥammadanism to Christ is one about which there can be no mistake. He is held to have been a great prophet, but to have been superseded by Muḥammad. His Deity, His atoning death, His claims to men's homage at the present day, are all scouted. As for Christ's Deity, Muḥammad in one of the last Sûrahs which he composed, states his opinion in these terrible but unmistakable words, "Verily[2] they have blasphemed who have said, Truly God is the Messiah, Son of Mary. Say thou, Who then could urge

[1] The influence of such men as Sayyid Aḥmad in India, whose Christian teaching and Western civilisation have greatly affected the opinions of the most educated Muslims, has produced a party of Neo-Muḥammadans, who, professing to be orthodox Muslims, strive to regenerate their decaying faith by importing into it much that is borrowed from the West. But all genuine Muslims feel great distrust of the movement, believing it unorthodox. Though the able men at the head of this movement are, through the 'Alîgaṛh College principally, gradually leavening Indian Muḥammadanism, they must not be regarded as representing genuine Muḥammadan ideas, any more than the leaders of the Brahmo Samāj can claim to represent Hindūism.

[2] Sûrah v. 19.

anything against God, if He wished to destroy the Messiah, son of Mary, and His people, and all that are in the world?"

Space will not permit us to dwell on the unscientific cosmogony, the innate intolerance, the antichristian character of Islâm. Muḥammad discovered not a single new truth, nor did he inculcate one single moral precept which had not been much more forcibly taught in the Old Testament. The loftier morality and the completed revelation of God contained in the New Testament, and above all in Christ Himself, he deliberately neglected or set aside. Instead of being an advance on Christianity therefore, as it claims to be, Islâm has retrograded far behind the limit reached by the Prophets of Israel. It has lost much that God had previously revealed, and has gained instead only heathen and Rabbinical myths, Jewish Pharisaism, and the Arabian fatalism and love of war. It is entirely destitute of proof. In spite, therefore, of its many half-truths borrowed from other systems, the existence of which we Christian missionaries thankfully acknowledge, and upon which we base our attempts to induce Muslims to accept the full light of the Gospel, it is not too much to say that, in the life and character of its Founder, the "Chosen" of God, and His ideal for the human race (as Muslims hold), Islâm has preserved an enduring and ever active principle of corruption, degradation and decay.

PART III

CHRISTIANITY AND CHRISTIAN MISSIONS IN INDIA

CHAPTER I

EARLY CHRISTIANITY IN INDIA.

THE occurrence of Sanskṛit and Tamil words in the list of the treasures and curiosities brought from the East by Hiram's ships in Solomon's time, proves that at least as early as the eleventh century before our era, the Phoenicians had reached the continent of India.[1] The fact that the earliest forms of some of the letters of the Sanskṛit alphabet[2] known to us not a little resemble the corresponding Phoenician characters, shows that those ancient mariners and traders had considerable and probably long continued intercourse with the Indian Âryans, just as they had with those of Hellas. While

[1] The fact that Homer uses the word κασσίτερος (from the Sanskṛit *kastîram*, tin), proves that in very ancient times the Ionian Greeks had some, doubtless indirect, intercourse with India.

[2] Professor Bühler has shown that there were two different kinds of script used in India in ancient times, the *Kharoshṭhî* and the *Brāhmî*. The former, used in the Gandhāra country (Eastern Afghānistān, and the North of the Panjāb), was derived from the Aramaic, and was in use from about B.C. 400 to A.D. 200, being always written from right to left. All the present alphabets of India are derived from the Brāhmî. This was usually written from left to right, but originally ran from right to left. This character is based on the oldest Phoenician script. Dr. Bühler believes that it was introduced into India by traders through Mesopotamia about B.C. 800 (*vide* Dr. Macdonell's *Hist. of Sanskrit Literature*, pp. 15, 16).

therefore it is impossible to state definitely at how early a period India became known to the Semites, it is at least well known that the conquests of Alexander first opened up India to any degree to the Western World. Pharaoh Necho[1] and Darius had, one after the other, begun and finished the canal which united the Red Sea with the waters of the Nile. The great Macedonian city of Alexandria in Egypt became the link of union between the countries bordering on the Mediterranean and those that lay on the shores of the Indian Ocean. A little later we are told that every year a Roman fleet of more than a hundred merchant vessels left the Arabian port of Myos Hormos at the summer solstice for Ceylon and Malabar, bringing thence pearls, spices, jewels and even the silks of China. Though we can hardly affirm the correctness of the view that the "Judaea" mentioned in Acts ii. 9 was actually an Indian region, yet there can be no doubt that, even in apostolic times,[2] Jewish converts and other Eastern Christians carried the good news of the coming of the promised Messiah to the western coast of India, between Baroch and Cape Comorin. The discovery, in A.D. 50, of the monsoons of the Indian Ocean gave new impetus to the trade between India and Egypt; and tradition, both Jewish and Christian, states that many of the Jews who were scattered from Jerusalem when that city was destroyed by Titus in A.D. 70, found a refuge in the trading settlements of their race in Western India, in Bombay and Cochin, where their descendants exist unto this day. Doubtless those of them who had embraced the Gospel, fired with Pentecostal zeal, endeavoured to spread their faith there, at least among their own countrymen. Thus was Christianity first preached in that distant land.

The belief of the Syrian Christians of St. Thomas in Malabar, that their Church was founded by that apostle himself, is not shared by any European scholar of repute. But the very existence of the tradition, and of the community in question, proves that India received Christian teachers in very early times from another quarter also, that is to say from Syria, and particularly from Edessa, which city is also said by both Syrian and Armenian historians to have heard the Gospel message from St. Thomas himself or from his converts. Antioch also sent forth missionaries to the distant East.

[1] Herodotus, ii. 158.

[2] George Smith, *Conversion of India*, pp. 8, 9.

The earliest missionary to India, however, whose name is recorded in history, came from Alexandria. His disciples, Clement and Origen, unite with Jerome and Eusebius in telling us how Pantaenus, Principal of the Christian College in that city, was sent to India by the Bishop of Alexandria, between A.D. 180 and 190, in response to an appeal from certain Indian Christians. At this we cannot wonder when we read of the zeal and repute of the man, and remember how Dion Chrysostom informs us that "Ethiopians, Arabians, Bactrians, Scythians, Persians and Indians" used at that time to flock to Alexandria, then the great seat of Western learning and the meeting-place of East and West. But it was not only to build up Christians in the faith that Pantaenus left Egypt, for Jerome expressly states that he "was sent to India that he might preach Christ among the Brāhmaṇs." In India he is said to have found in use the Hebrew Gospel of St. Matthew, which tradition affirmed had been given to the Christian community there by the Apostle Bartholemew. We know not what success attended Pantaenus' efforts, but we are told that he ultimately returned to Alexandria.

We hear nothing further of Christianity in India until Theophilus Indicus came to Europe from Socotra in Constantine's time. On his way he had visited India, where he found a flourishing Christian Church. At the Nicene Council in A.D. 325 we find present the Metropolitan of Persia and "of the Great India," whose name was John.

Connected as they always had been with Syria, we are not surprised that the Christians of India readily received Nestorian missionaries from Seleucia-Ctesiphon, when, early in the sixth century, the Nestorian Church began its great and far-reaching evangelistic work. At Madras and in Travancore crosses with Syriac and Pahlavī inscriptions, dating from the seventh century, have been found.[1] The Nestorians preached the Gospel along the whole of the Western coast of India, and as far as Ceylon. Cosmas Indicopleustes, writing in A.D. 547, tells us of the extent to which Christianity had even then been propagated in the East. "Even in the island of Taprobanê (Ceylon), in Farther India, where the Indian Sea is," he writes,[2] "there is a church of Christians, with clergy and a congregation of believers, though I know not if there be any Christians farther

[1] *Indian Antiquary*, Nov. 1874.

[2] Quoted by George Smith, *op. cit.* p. 29.

on in that direction; and such is also the case in the land called Malê, where the pepper grows. And in the place called Calliana[1] there is a bishop, appointed from Persia, as well as in the isle called the Isle of Dioscoris in the same Indian Sea. The inhabitants of that island speak Greek, having been originally settled there by the Ptolemies, who ruled after Alexander of Macedon. There are clergy there also, ordained and sent from Persia to minister among the people of the island, and a multitude of Christians."

According to the census of 1891, out of the total Christian population of 2,284,172 then in India, no fewer than 200,467 belonged to the Syrian Church. They are to be found chiefly in Cochin, and are the descendants of the early Indian Christians of whom Cosmas speaks. It is clear therefore that though, during the Dark Ages, the Christians of India, cut off from the West by the Muḥammadan conquest of Persia, Mesopotamia, Syria, Egypt and other ancient seats of Christian learning, had in many places fallen away from the faith, and been absorbed into the surrounding mass of heathenism, yet the toil of the early preachers of the Gospel in India cannot be said to have been in vain. In our own time, too, many of the Syrian Christians have cast off the accretions to their faith which had gradually overspread their Church, and have returned to a purer and more apostolic Christianity. This is due, under God, to the new light brought to India by Christian missionaries from Europe and America. It is interesting to learn that our first connexion with Indian Christianity was due to King Alfred, who in the year 883 sent an embassy under Sighelm, bishop of Shireburn, to St. Thomas' shrine at Madras.[2]

[1] Probably Kalyân, near Bombay.
[2] So says Thomas of Malmesbury.

CHAPTER II

ROMAN CATHOLIC MISSIONS IN INDIA.

BETWEEN the time of Cosmas Indicopleustes and the beginning of Roman Catholic missionary work in India, we know but little of the state of the Christian Church in that country. Visitors and travellers from the West, however, give us a few glimpses of it. Ḥethoum I., king of the small Armenian sovereignty of Cilicia, during his four years' journey to the court of Mungû Khân at Qaraqorum (A.D. 1252–55), wrote a letter to the king and queen of Cyprus, his near relations, in which he mentions a Christian king in India, whose people had been freed from the tyranny of the Muḥammadans by the conquests of Chingîz Khân and his successors. The next information which we have on the subject is due to Marco Polo, the Venetian traveller, who, holding a position of some importance under Qublai Khân, paid three visits to that country. On his first visit he came from Yûnnân to the province of "Bangala," which then included not only part of Bengal, but also Burma and Assam. Somewhat later he spent some time in different parts of the South of India. Finally, when leaving Cathay for the court of Arghûn, king of Persia, he again passed along the coast, visiting Ceylon and various other places, including Malabar, Socotra and Mekrân. This traveller informs us that, towards the close of the thirteenth century, Christians and Jews were found in most of the following eleven districts, Telingāna, Madras, Tanjore, Tinnevelly, Comorin, Quilon, Kananor, Bombay, Cambay, Somnāth and Mekrân. He states that the Christians of Socotra were independent of Rome, and were governed by an archbishop appointed by the Syrian Metrân at Baudas (Baghdâd). But Christianity soon afterwards so degenerated in the island that a Carmelite monk on his visit to the place found that the people, though showing reverence for the Cross and calling themselves Christians, not only practised circumcision, but also offered sacrifices to the moon. The island is now wholly abandoned to Muḥammadanism.

John of Monte Corvino, whom the Pope appointed Archbishop of Peking and Patriarch of a large part of the Eastern world, was the first to begin Roman Catholic mission work in India, early in the fourteenth century. He was followed by a man of great missionary zeal and devotion, a Dominican friar named Jordanus. Sent out by the Pope, who then resided at Avignon, Jordanus and his companions passed through Persia to Hormuz and sailed thence to Diu, whence they proceeded to Thāna near Bombay, landing there in A.D. 1321. At that time that part of India was in the hands of the Muḥammadans. While Jordanus was away on a preaching tour in the north, four Franciscan missionaries, Thomas, James, Demetrius and Peter, were martyred for maintaining the Deity of our Lord. Jordanus has left us two letters, in one of which he urges the missionaries at Tabrîz to send men to work at Surat, Baroch and Quilon. After working for a year at Quilon, Jordanus returned to Europe, and was sent forth again in A.D. 1330 by Pope John XXII. as bishop, commended to the Christians of India by a Papal bull, which invited the Syrian Church of that country to submit to the Roman See. Jordanus does not speak in high terms of the scattered Syrians of India, but he tells us that the heathen permitted him to make converts without opposition, and of the earnestness of his converts he speaks in high terms. He claims to have baptized some 300 persons, some of whom seem to have been converts from Islâm. From the Muḥammadans, however, Jordanus received most determined opposition, and endured a great deal of persecution, though he was denied the crown of martyrdom to which he most eagerly aspired, and which was gained by nine of his missionary brethren, four of whom were the Martyrs of Thāna.

The work thus begun by Italian missionaries was continued by the Portuguese, though it soon degenerated into a system of the most terrible tyranny and persecution.

Vasco da Gama rounded the Cape of Good Hope in 1497, and thus opened up a new way to India. After a voyage of eleven months' duration he landed at Calicut on the 20th May 1498. The infamous Pope, Alexander Borgia, had appointed the king of Portugal "Lord of the Navigation, Conquest and Trade of Ethiopia, Arabia, Persia and India." On Da Gama's second visit he was saluted as their ruler by the Christians of Malabar. Albuquerque and Almeida, the first Portuguese viceroy, gradually laid the foundation of the Portuguese Empire in India. But the vices of the nominal Christians who came from Portugal prevented the spread of the faith. Nothing of importance from a missionary point of view was done until the arrival of the great and devoted Jesuit missionary Francis Xavier, who landed in Goa in 1542. For the next three years he toiled as a missionary there and in the neighbouring parts of the country. He then devoted two years and a half to a visit to the numerous islands in the Chinese seas. Returning to India, he spent four years more in the work of superintending and directing the various Jesuit missions in different parts of India, and in a visit to Japan. After residing two years in that country he returned once more to Goa. He died in the island of Sancian, near Canton, on the 2nd December 1552, while endeavouring to reach Peking, with the hope of gaining permission from the emperor to establish a mission in China.

Xavier was himself a man of deep spirituality, and possessed by an earnest love of souls. But the defective system of religion to which he owned allegiance made him believe in the efficacy of mere outward rites and ceremonies, without any change of heart. Hence he toiled unceasingly to baptize newly-born children, but he seems never to have learned to speak any of the vernacular languages of the different tribes and peoples to whom he preached. He appears at length to have felt that his work was not a success, and he recommends just two methods for the conversion of India,—the baptism and subsequent instruction of the native children, and the use of force. Hence in November 1545 he entreated John III., king of Portugal, to introduce into Goa and Portuguese India generally the infamous institution known as the "Holy Office." This was not done, however, until some years later.

The Abbé Dubois, about a hundred years ago, writing about Xavier's work, sums up his account in the following words: "At last Francis Xavier, entirely disheartened by the innumerable obstacles he everywhere met in his apostolic career, and by the apparent impossibility of making real converts, left the country in disgust."

The Inquisition was established in Goa in 1560, principally with the object of putting down Judaism, which, as we have already seen, had existed in Western and Southern India from the times of the destruction of the Second Temple of Jerusalem. The terrible institution continued to burn and torture not the Jews only, but other heretics also, until it was finally abolished, through British influence, in 1816.

Xavier does not seem to have endeavoured to interfere to any extent with the Syrian Christians whom he found in India. But the first bishop of Goa, a Franciscan named Don Juan d'Albuquerque, began to attack that ancient Church in 1545, with the purpose of forcing it to bow to the Papal yoke. The Jesuits continued the campaign; and at last Philip II. of Spain, having become monarch of Portugal and its dependencies, sent Don Aleixo de Menezes to Goa as archbishop, with the object of accomplishing the task. The Metran and other high dignitaries of the Nestorian Church were most cruelly treated, but their people bravely resisted their rulers' tyranny. In 1595 Pope Clement VIII. gave Menezes plenary power to work his will. The engines of the Inquisition were brought into operation against not only the Syrians, but all others also whom the Inquisitors regarded as hostile to Rome. The Muḥammadans, amongst others, were subjected to a cruel persecution, and many of them thrown into the dungeon or put to death. At last the archbishop compelled the archdeacon, who was the only remaining head of the Syrian Church, to attend a synod at Diamper in 1599, and, by privately signing a certain document, to renounce for himself and his Church their ancestral allegiance to the patriarch of Babylon, and submit to Rome. From this forced submission the Syrian Church was delivered by the Dutch, when in 1663 they took Cochin and overthrew the Portuguese power in the East.

Acknowledging the comparative failure of both Xavier and the Inquisition, the Jesuits who succeeded the former in his work determined to make a new beginning and to adopt an entirely different plan. Robert de Nobilibus, Cardinal Bellarmine's nephew, obtaining the approval of the archbishop of Cranganor to his scheme, went to Madura on the eastern coast of Southern India, then the capital of King Tirumala, and there pretended to be a Brāhmaṇ prince from Rome and a strict Hindū ascetic (*sanyāsī*). Clad in the yellow robe and with the sacred heathen mark in sandal-wood stamped on his forehead, he received those who, impelled by curiosity, came to see him, and, speaking to them in their native Tamil, taught them a strangely heterogeneous mixture of Hindūism and Roman Catholicism. His influence spread so widely that thousands became his followers, and he was delighted by his success in surreptitiously baptizing dying infants. At last the Brāhmaṇs, jealous of the influence he had gained over the king, and fearing the loss of their own wealth and honours, dethroned the king, and in 1693 began a religious persecution. Robert de Nobilibus was imitated by many others, one of the most famous of whom was a Portuguese noble named John Hector de Brito. This able but misguided man actually took an oath before the Brāhmaṇs that he belonged to their caste, and forged the fifth or *Ezour* Veda to enable him to introduce what he believed to be the main doctrines of Christianity in this disguise among the Hindūs. He also composed certain Tamil works with the same object. After toiling for forty-two years in this way, he was driven from Madura to Ceylon, and at last died at Madras. Even Menezes, who thought few deeds too evil to be justifiable in the cause of religion, was shocked at the impiety of this plan of the Jesuits. A second persecution was directed against their deluded followers in Madura in the year 1714; but Beschi, another most learned Jesuit, revived the work there a little later. When at last the deception was discovered and blazoned abroad, thousands of the deluded converts returned to the Hindū religion from which they had been seduced. The discovery was in large measure due to the Franciscans and Dominicans, who had always been rivals of the Jesuit order. Pope Gregory XV. was deluded into permitting certain of the evil practices adopted by the Jesuits. But the scandal at last grew so notorious that, after the failure of several attempts made by the Papal See to amend matters, Pope Benedict XIV. in 1745 issued a bull which brought the whole disgraceful business to a conclusion. This was soon after followed by the suppression of the Jesuits for a time.

Roman Catholic missionaries found their way to the Emperor Akbar's court at Âgra, where they succeeded in gaining some slight, temporary influence. They entered Nipāl in 1661.

After the occupation of the Jaffna province of Ceylon by the Portuguese in 1548, the Roman Catholics used worldly inducements to prevail on the people to submit to baptism.

These means succeeded there far better than in India proper,—so well, in fact, that within a few years almost the whole population became nominal Christians. But, as they had little or no Christian teaching, they for the most part continued to practise heathen and Buddhist rites in private, and were ready to renounce their professed Christianity when an opportunity came.

The overthrow of the Portuguese power by the Dutch in India in 1663, and in Ceylon in 1658, almost put a stop to Roman Catholic missionary work in those countries. At the present time it is carried on hardly at all, if at all, among either heathen or Muḥammadans, though in certain places attempts are made from time to time to utilise any dissensions among the members of native Protestant Churches in order to lead them to enter the Roman Catholic fold. Yet the descendants of Xavier's converts are so numerous that the Roman Catholic native Christians in India in 1891 amounted to about one and a quarter million of souls. The corrupt and merely nominal Christianity of many of these persons often brings discredit on their Christian profession, and is the main reason why Europeans think they have grounds for condemning Christian servants as often more dishonest and unscrupulous than Hindū and Muḥammadan ones. Comparatively few Protestant native Christians are to be found as the servants of Europeans.

CHAPTER III

MISSIONS UNDER THE DUTCH, AND THE EAST INDIA COMPANY.

THE first good effect of the overthrow of Portuguese power by the Dutch in Western India, was the liberation of the Syrian Church from its compulsory submission to Rome. Part, indeed, of the Syrian community still continued to profess Roman Catholicism, and they are incorrectly styled the Old Church or Catholics of the Syrian rite. But the greater part of the community, deprived of their connexion with Moṣul, became united to the Jacobite Church of Antioch, as they still continue to be. Their first bishop, consecrated by the Patriarch of Antioch, was Mar Gregorius; and under its new government their Church dates from 1665.

Although the Dutch originally determined that their Presbyterian Church should rise to the dignity of the Divine call which it had received to carry the pure and simple gospel of Christ to the people of India, Ceylon and the Eastern Archipelago, yet they can hardly be said as a nation to have done their duty in the matter. Among their ranks, it is true, some great and devoted missionaries were found; but the Dutch East India Company cannot claim to have done more for the cause of Christ than, as we shall see, the English East India Company afterwards did. Both these great mercantile communities in different ways hindered, rather than assisted, the spread of Christianity among their subjects.

The chief Dutch settlements in India proper were at Cochin, Negapatam, Palakollu, Sadras and Chinsurah. The faith of the Reformed Church of Holland was in 1642 established as the religion of Palakollu, and the Dutch began to persecute the Roman Catholics. Baldaeus and two other Dutch missionaries in the province of Jaffna in Ceylon were soon able to report that they had converted more than 180,000 heathen. A proclamation was published in the Southern province of the island compelling the Buddhists there to become baptized, and refusing all public offices, and even permission to practise agriculture, to any who were not communicant members of the Church. As a natural consequence multitudes outwardly professed Christianity, though there were not teachers enough to instruct them in the very first principles of the faith. The result of this was seen when the English conquered Dutch India in 1782 and Ceylon in 1796. Although there were then nearly 500,000 professing native Protestant Christians in Ceylon alone, they had only 14 clergy to minister to them. When the converts found that their new rulers professed religious neutrality, they almost without exception relapsed into their ancient religions, in which they had never really ceased to believe. Claudius Buchanan in 1806 visited the island, and stated that Protestantism had there ceased to exist among the natives. The Dutch had neglected to give the people the Bible in their vernacular tongues, and even the missionaries had in too many cases omitted to learn the native languages, contenting themselves with preaching through interpreters. Can we wonder that their work so completely failed? Nor is there any room to doubt that the Dutch lost their Eastern empire, in God's providence, because they had been unfaithful to their sacred trust, and in their haste to enrich themselves had not cared to adopt the proper methods for handing on to their subjects those great truths which their fathers, not long before, had purchased with their blood.

As is well known, the British Empire in India was founded by the East India Company. This great mercantile association, incorporated in 1599,—the year that witnessed the extinction of the liberty of the Syrian Church in India,—received its first charter from Elizabeth on the 31st December 1600. It was founded merely for trading purposes, and with no higher object began a career which lasted for more than two centuries and a half. Although the Company provided a few chaplains for the benefit of its European agents in India, and afterwards tolerated such missionaries as Schwartz and Kiernander, yet the first English church was not begun in India until 1681, 81 years after the Company's formation. The conduct of the great mass of the English in India in those days was such as to lead the natives to believe that Christianity was the religion of the devil, or that Europeans had no religion whatever.

In the charter granted to the "English Company" in 1698, the provisions of which were applied to the East India Company also when the two associations became united in 1708, it was laid down that clergy, approved by the Archbishop of Canterbury or the Bishop of London, should be sent out as chaplains. They were directed to learn Portuguese, and to study the vernacular, "the better to enable them to instruct the Gentoos, that shall be the servants or slaves of the same Company, or of their agents, in the Protestant religion." Missionary work was therefore distinctly contemplated, at least to a limited extent. But the number of chaplains was very limited, and they were not always men of the best character.

During the time of Clive and Warren Hastings, when the Company carried on the military operations which changed their directors into the rulers of a great empire, things went from bad to worse. Vice and irreligion were rampant almost everywhere. Few cared to attend Divine service when it was held, and frequently the chaplains were not permitted to discharge their functions at all. Even somewhat later than this, Dr. Claudius Buchanan, when for three years he was chaplain to the troops at Barrackpore, twelve miles from Calcutta, was not once permitted to preach except in his own house. Englishmen for the most part lived in India as if they had only one article in their creed, to wit, the proverb which, in a somewhat later form, states that the Ten Commandments cease to be in force beyond the Isthmus of Suez.

All through the eighteenth century, however, missionary work was being carried on to a limited extent in the Southern part of India. This was begun by Ziegenbalg and Plutscho in the Tamil country, under the patronage of Frederick IV. of Denmark. That monarch in 1705 remembered that the Danish East India Company had traded with India for ninety years, during which time many of their merchants had resided at their settlement at Tranquebar, and yet, though Danish governors and soldiers had been sent out to govern and defend the territory in question, no Danish missionary had ever gone forth thither to preach the word of God. He therefore educated, trained, and sent out at his own expense the two men named above. Ziegenbalg translated the New and part of the Old Testament into Tamil, and laboured most earnestly and with much success as a missionary. Schwartz, who went to India in 1749, was one of the greatest heralds of the Gospel in modern times. Under him the work of the mission spread throughout the country from Madras to Tinnevelly, and many converts entered the fold. The work soon came entirely under the control of the English Society for Promoting Christian Knowledge, though the missionaries continued to come from Germany. More than 50,000 converts were baptized before the close of the century. Schwartz's own influence was immense and unique. He was known far and wide as "the Christian," and was chosen under that title by Ḥaidar 'Alî, Râjâ of Mysore, as the only emissary from the British whom he could trust. But Schwartz and his fellow-labourers were too hasty in admitting men to baptism, and in permitting the retention of caste among their converts they made a very great mistake. Hence, soon after Schwartz's death in 1798, many of the converts relapsed into heathenism, and the work languished until it was taken up by the Society for the Propagation of the Gospel during last century.

Protestant missions in the North of India owe their origin to Kiernander, another Danish missionary, whom Clive invited to Calcutta from Tranquebar in 1758. He built the Old Church in Calcutta in 1771. His work lay principally among the Portuguese and Eurasians, though he also baptized a few heathen converts.

From the year 1793, when William Wilberforce failed to induce the English Parliament to insert in the East India Company's charter certain clauses drawn up with a view to facilitate missionary work in their territories, until 1813, the Company did all they could to thwart every effort to spread the Gospel in India. When Carey, the great Baptist missionary, reached Bengal in 1793, he had to have his name entered as an indigo-planter and go inland in that capacity, in order to avoid being expelled from British India. As Mr. Eugene Stock[1] well says: "There, and in that capacity, lived for six years the one representative in India of the missionary zeal of Christian England; and in that obscure—one may say ignominious—way began English missions in her great dependency."

In 1799 four other missionaries managed to reach Calcutta by taking passage in an American vessel. But they were

[1] *History of the C.M.S.* vol. i. p. 96.

instantly ordered to leave the country, and would have had to do so but for the fact that there existed at Serampore, some fifteen miles up the Hūghlī, a small Danish settlement. Escaping thither by night, they were protected by the Danish governor, who refused to surrender them when summoned to do so by the Government of Calcutta. When Carey heard this good news, he at once left his indigo-planting and joined his brethren at Serampore. Thus in January 1800 was the mission in that place founded, and a work begun which was to have the most widespread effects on India for all future time.

Claudius Buchanan, who in 1797 had reached Calcutta as a chaplain, had already obtained great influence by his preaching and Christian character. He was soon, with David Brown, placed at the head of the College of Fort William, founded by the Governor-General, Marquis Wellesley, for the purpose of affording young Englishmen instruction in the Indian languages. Brown induced the Governor to appoint Carey Professor of Bengali there. These three earnest Christian men devoted their large salaries in great measure to the preparation and printing of vernacular translations of the Bible.

Meanwhile the work at Serampore and in the surrounding country had been greatly blessed. Not only from Hindūs of the lower classes were converts won, but from the Brāhmaṇs and even from Muḥammadans. When, however, the work spread to Calcutta, it was quickly checked by the antichristian policy of the Government. But the latter, though opposing Christian missions, showed the false "liberality" which was then and is now so popular, by taking under its protection the Temple of Jagannāth.

The mutiny of some Sepoys at Vellore, near Madras, in 1806, was made an excuse for more determined opposition to missionary work. The enemies of Christ endeavoured, by loudly repeated assertions, to convince themselves as well as other people that the affair, like every other adverse event, was wholly due to the spread of the Gospel. In a similar manner the spiritual ancestors of these "candid critics" attributed the invasion of the barbarians in Augustine's time, together with all the other ills which then befell the Roman Empire, to the preaching of the Christian faith, and thus drew forth from Augustine that noble treatise on *The City of God*, which completely demolished their argument, if argument it can be called. Accordingly, when two Baptist missionaries arrived in

1807, they were at once expelled. In the providence of God this led to good results, for one of them went to Burma and there founded a flourishing mission. In 1812 the first five missionaries of the recently formed American Board of Commissioners of Foreign Missions reached Calcutta, but were not allowed to land. Two of them, of whom one was Judson, went to Burma and joined the Baptist Mission there. The other three managed to reach Bombay by sea, and they set on foot the extensive American Mission in Gujarât. Three English missionaries who arrived in Calcutta in the same year, and another who was working in Madras in connexion with the London Missionary Society, were also driven from the place, and indeed from the country.

But a change was at hand. When the East India Company's charter was renewed in 1813, the phenomenal efforts of Wilberforce, the two Charles Grants and other noble Christian men, secured the insertion in it of two clauses of the greatest importance to the cause of Christ. One of these provided for the creation of an ecclesiastical establishment in India, while the other enacted that measures should be adopted to introduce among the natives of British India "useful knowledge and religious and moral improvement." This was the dawn of better things and a brighter future for India. But only one man, an English schoolmaster, was actually sent out by the C.M.S.[1] in 1813; and the first Church of England clergymen to go as missionaries to Asia were despatched by the same Society in 1815.[2]

It must not, however, be forgotten that some among the Government chaplains in India, though prevented from devoting all their energies to missionary work, had, even during the dark period before 1813, done much to lay the foundation upon which future missions were built. The labours of Brown and Buchanan have already been briefly mentioned. Corrie, Thomason and above all the devoted Henry Martyn did much for the cause. Martyn's Urdū and Persian versions of the New Testament proved of the very greatest value. Martyn's convert from Islām, 'Abdu'l Masīḥ, began work in Âgra in 1813 under Corrie's supervision, and was ultimately the first Indian Church of England clergyman, being ordained by Bishop Heber in 1826.

In summing up the good work accomplished in India during

[1] Established in 1799. [2] Greenwood and Norton.

the first half of the nineteenth century in accordance with the Acts and Regulations of the East India Company, Dr. George Smith says:[1] "The Christlike work kept rapid step with the progress of Christian opinion and beneficent reforms in Great Britain, but it was due in the first instance to the missionaries in India. In the teeth of the supporters of Hindūism, European as well as Brāhmaṇical, and contrary to the custom of centuries, it ceased to be lawful, it became penal, even in the name of religion, (1) to murder parents by suttee, by exposure on the banks of rivers, or by burial alive; (2) to murder children by dedication to the Ganges, to be devoured by crocodiles, or daughters by the Rājpūt modes of infanticide; (3) to offer up human sacrifices in a temple, or to propitiate the earth-goddess; (4) to encourage suicide under the wheels of idol cars, or in wells, or otherwise; (5) to promote voluntary torment by hook-swinging, thigh-piercing, tongue-extraction, etc.; or (6) involuntary torment by mutilation, trampling to death, ordeals and barbarous executions. Slavery and the slave-trade were made illegal. Caste was no longer supported by law nor recognised in appointments to office. The long compromise with idolatry during the previous two centuries ceased, so that the Government no more called its Christian soldiers to salute idols, or its civil officers to recognise gods in official documents, or manage the affairs of idol temples, and extort a revenue from idol pilgrimages. A long step was taken by legislative acts to protect the civil rights of converts to Christianity as to any other religion, and to leave Hindū widows free to marry."

Any missionary work done in India, in spite of the opposition of the East India Company, before 1813 was merely preparatory. When, however, the new charter gave opportunities for preaching the Gospel, the various sections of the Church of Christ in Great Britain and the United States slowly but steadily set to work to enter in at the now open door. We have seen how the Church Missionary Society began its work. The S.P.C.K. and the S.P.G. took up the work in earnest also. Congregationalist and Baptist missionaries from the United States were sent in 1813, Wesleyan missionaries came to Mysore in 1817. The Established Church of Scotland sent out Alexander Duff in 1830, a man whose work has influenced the higher classes in Calcutta and the whole of Bengal—we might almost say the

[1] *The Conversion of India*, pp. 110, 111.

whole of India—more than that of anyone else from that time to the present. Donald Mitchell came to Bombay in 1823, Robert Nesbit and John Wilson in 1835. The latter baptized the first Pārsī converts in 1839. The Wilson College is still exercising a vast influence for good in Bombay. Work was begun in Madras and South India in 1837. The Disruption of the Scottish Church in 1843 imparted new life to the two new organisations, the Free and the Established Churches, which may be said to have originated therefrom. The Free Church retained and carried on more vigorously than ever the work already commenced, while new missions in the Panjāb, Darjeeling and elsewhere were undertaken by the Established Church, which also continued the work at Calcutta and Madras. The Baptists also began a great work in Northern India. In 1829 the S.P.G. undertook direct missionary work among the heathen, and took over the work of the German missionaries in the South from the S.P.C.K. At the request of a chaplain, the Rev. Jas. Hough, the Church Missionary Society in 1820 sent Rhenius and Schmid to Palamcotta. The same Society began work among the Syrian Christians at Cottayam in 1817, at Allepie in the previous year, and at Cochin in 1817. Henry Baker and Joseph Fenn arrived in 1818. Their object was not to destroy but to reform the ancient Syrian Church, and through it extend the preaching of the Gospel among the surrounding heathen. But, though the Metrans at first welcomed their assistance, opposition ultimately arose, and in 1825 a new Metran began a counter movement, which, in 1836, led the C.M.S. to retire from the attempt to renovate the Syrian Church, and to devote all their energies to the conversion of the heathen. In this they were aided by not a few Syrians who had been enlightened, and could no longer tolerate the corruptions to which their own Church had become wedded. Noble and Fox began a great work in and around Masulipatam in 1841; and in 1850 the Society took up the task of preaching the Gospel to the Pahārī or mountain tribes of Rājmaḥall.

A new and most important development of the work began in 1834, when for the first time an association, afterwards named the Society for Promoting Female Education in the East (the "F.E.S."), was founded to carry the Gospel message to the women of India. Not a few devoted wives of missionaries had previously laboured among the wives and daughters of converts, but they were quite unable to do all that had to be done.

Among Muḥammadan women in particular it was impossible for male missionaries to work; and the influence of Muḥammadanism had rendered the seclusion of Hindū women necessary to a much greater extent than had been customary before the Muḥammadan conquests in the country. From that time to this the work among women carried on by the F.E.S. and somewhat later undertaken also by the Baptist Zenana Mission, the Indian Female Normal School Society, now known as the Zenana Bible and Medical Mission, the C.E.Z.M.S., the C.M.S. and other societies, has continued to be greatly blessed.

The London Missionary Society was at work in Bengal and still more extensively in Southern India, long before the abolition of the East India Company. In 1834 began the labours of the Basel Mission in Malabar and those of the American Board of Missions in Madura. The American Baptist Telugu Mission was started in 1835, and those of the American Presbyterians in the North-West Provinces in 1836. In 1841 the Leipzig Lutheran Mission in the Carnatic, the Irish Presbyterian Mission in Gujarāt, the Welsh Calvinistic Methodist in Bengal, and the Berlin Mission in Bihār, were all alike founded. Gossner's Mission to the Kōls began in 1846. The work begun by the C.M.S. in 1818 in Ceylon had been carried on steadily amid much discouragement, but it was not until later times that it bore much visible fruit. Missionaries were sent there by the Wesleyan Missionary Society in 1813.

The first really successful Medical Mission in India was set on foot by Dr. H. M. Scudder of the Dutch Reformed Church of America in 1850 among the people of North Arcot, but the immense value of that department of missionary energy was not recognised until much later. The same year saw the establishment of a C.M.S. Mission at Karāchī, and also Lord Dalhousie's grant of tolerance to converts from any one faith to any other. This was a great step in advance, since it relieved native Christians from the very heavy legal disabilities under which they had until that time laboured.

Dr. Mullens and Mr. Sherring reckon the total number of native Protestant Christians in India, Burma and Ceylon in 1830 at about 27,000. The progress of missionary work from that time until the Mutiny was so great that in May 1857 they probably amounted to 130,000, drawn from all classes and creeds, from the highest castes to the very lowest.

In the Mutiny the Indian Church had many noble martyrs

and confessors, especially because the mutineers identified them with the ruling race against whose power they had risen in rebellion. Among those who won the martyr's crown may be mentioned Wilāyat 'Alī, Thakūr, Dhokul Parshād, Paramānand, Solomon, Rāmchandra Mitra, Jīwan Masīḥ, Raphael, Dr. Chaman Lāl, and many others. "The Muḥammadans always, and the Hindūs occasionally, offered such their lives at the price of denying their Lord. Not one instance can be cited of failure to confess Him by men and women, very often of weak physique, and but yesterday of the same faith as their murderers."[1]

[1] George Smith, *Conversion of India*, p. 138.

CHAPTER IV

MISSIONS IN INDIA SINCE THE MUTINY.

When the terrible Indian Mutiny of 1857 had been finally suppressed and order restored, the East India Company's territory became the Indian Empire under the direct control of the British Parliament. Queen Victoria's Proclamation to that effect became law in August of that year, and was publicly read aloud at Government House, Calcutta, on the 1st November. This Proclamation, while clearly stating the Queen's reliance on the truth of Christianity, promised to her subjects of all beliefs alike "the equal and impartial protection of the law," and forbade all who should hold authority under her to interfere in any way with the religious belief or worship of any of her subjects. This declaration has always since been interpreted as binding the Government of India to observe strict neutrality in religious matters. Although attempts have been made from time to time by the enemies of Christianity to hinder certain departments of mission work, yet on the whole the Indian Government has loyally observed the spirit as well as the letter of the Act, and as a result missionary work has been much aided by the straightforward and righteous Christian policy thus outlined.

The lurid light shed upon the condition of India by the Mutiny, and the increased knowledge of and interest in the country thus produced, led many Christians in the United Kingdom and in America to perceive what great responsibilities were laid upon the English by the possession of India, and to resolve to endeavour to perform the duties arising therefrom. New energy was diffused into every missionary society already labouring in India, and fresh organisations were formed to enable the many open doors to be entered. The Christian Vernacular Education Society, now known as the Christian

Literature Society for India, began its work as at once a memorial of the Mutiny and a token of gratitude to God for its suppression. The Methodist Episcopal Church of America, acting on Dr. Duff's advice, sent labourers to toil for Christ in Oudh and Rohilk'hand. The missionaries of the United Presbyterian Church of Scotland, at Dr. Wilson's suggestion, turned their attention to the tribes of Rājpūtāna. The Moravians, the Society of Friends, the Original Secession Church of Scotland, the Presbyterian Church of Canada and other smaller bodies of Christians, started missions in various parts of British India. The "Comity of Missions," an arrangement by which the various Protestant societies undertake not to enter one another's fields without an invitation to do so from those already labouring in any particular district, had long previously been acted upon and had prevented much waste of energy. It has been found in India by practical experience that the various matters of Church order and even of doctrine, which separate one body of Protestants from another, however important they may seem to some, sink into insignificance in the presence of the unmentionable abominations of heathenism and the blasphemies of Muḥammadanism. It is practically upon this basis that the Comity of Missions rests, and the practical result is thus to bring nearer the time when the longing desire of the dying Saviour shall be accomplished, that "they all may be one" in Him, so that the world may believe and bow to His claims to be the Saviour of the world.

One sign of the consciousness of unity which working side by side with one another in the mission field produces among evangelical Christians is afforded by the Week of Universal Prayer. In the autumn of 1859 the American missionaries at Lūdhiāna in the Panjāb sent out an invitation to Christians everywhere to unite in prayer for the outpouring of God's Holy Spirit on the Christian Church at large. This was first begun in January 1860, and has been observed ever since. The blessings vouchsafed in reply have been manifold, but the first evident token that the believing prayer had been heard was the memorable revival in Tinnevelly in March 1860.

The American Presbyterian Mission had occupied one or two stations in the Panjāb in 1845 and 1849 after the first and second Sikh Wars respectively. At the invitation of some

Christian officers, seconded by the American missionaries Newton and Forman, then in Lahore, the Church Missionary Society occupied Amritsar in 1851. One of the first two missionaries sent thither, the Rev. Robert Clark, was spared to see the Panjāb Native Church become one of the most vigorous and flourishing in the whole of India. Peshāwar was occupied in 1855, Multān in 1856. But the great extension of the work in the Panjāb, as in nearly every other part of India, began shortly after the Mutiny, to the suppression of which the Sikh troops so materially contributed.

In 1860 an important work among the Santāls, one of the aboriginal hill-tribes of Bengal, was begun by the C.M.S. This is but one instance of the efforts made to reach the numerous tribes in different parts of India who are quite distinct from the Hindūs, and, having no caste and no very definite system of religion, are more accessible to the Gospel than those whom pride of ancestry and race tends to prevent from humbly receiving it like little children. Work is now carried on by various societies among Kōls, Santāls, Bhīls, Gōnds, Hill Arrians and many other such tribes.

The work in India has now grown to such dimensions that it is quite impossible in the limited space at our command to dwell upon even the most important missions of the many societies which are engaged in the work. It remains, however, to give some account of the leading methods of evangelisation employed and to show something of the results which have already, by God's blessing and by the agency of His Holy Spirit, been attained. The various general conferences of all Protestant missions at work in the country, which have been held at intervals of ten years for a considerable time past, enable these different branches of the one Church of Christ to co-operate with one another, and to discuss the best methods of working. Hence there is a general agreement in such methods; and though, for example, the higher educational work is carried on more particularly by the Free and the Established Church of Scotland, the Zenana work by the F.E.S. and the C.E.Z.M.S., and literary work by the Christian Literature Society, yet no society has the monopoly of any single department. The Calcutta Missionary Conference in 1890 reported that there were then 64 different societies, great and small, at work in various parts of India, Ceylon and Burma. Eighteen of these belong to the United States, and 17 to Germany and other Continental countries.

One of the most important methods by which all Protestant societies endeavour to evangelise the world is by translating Holy Scripture into the various languages of the nations. When Carey began his work at Serampore, the Bible existed only in some 30 languages, but before his death it had already appeared in some 40 more. Many of the versions made by Carey, Marshman and others of that day were only tentative, but who can say to how many souls they, even in that form, brought the Light of Life? These early translations have served as the basis for others; fresh ones have been made; and now, among the 103 languages and dialects of India, there is not one of the first importance that does not own a good version of the Bible, while the New Testament, or at least the Gospels, have been translated into nearly all. Many of these languages were unwritten until the arrival of the Christian missionary. While the missionaries of the various societies make such versions with the best native assistance available, the British and Foreign Bible Society, and to a lesser degree other similar associations, undertake the task of printing, publishing and circulating the versions thus produced. When we remember that one of the chief reasons for the ultimate failure of the Nestorian, Roman Catholic and Dutch missions in India, Persia, China and other lands, was their failure to give their converts the Bible in the vernacular languages, we can the better understand the immense value, nay the imperative necessity, of the great work of Bible translation which has distinguished the nineteenth Christian century.

Closely connected with this is the work of producing a Christian vernacular literature. It is not too much to say that Arabic, Persian, Urdū, Hindī and many other languages hardly contain a single work fit to be placed in the hands of the female portion of the community, except the books of Christian missionaries and of native Christian converts. The writings of such men as Bābā Padmanjī and Ganpatrāo in Marāṭhī, 'Imādu'd Dīn in Urdū, Lāl Behārī Dey in Bengālī, not to mention very many others in Tamil, Telugu, Malayālim, Gujarātī and other tongues, are of the greatest value. English, too, has been and is being extensively used by Dr. Murdoch and his associates. Dr. Pfander's works in Persian, Arabic and Urdū have laid the axe to the root of the tree of

Islām.[1] The missionaries in India have again and again urged upon their societies individually and collectively the necessity of assigning able men to this particular branch of work, that is to say, the production of a vernacular Christian literature. It is to be hoped that in the near future the task will be far more systematically undertaken than it has ever yet been.

We have already briefly referred to the commencement of Zenana and medical mission work in India. These are of very great value. Medical missionaries are obeying to the letter our Lord's command to His first disciples to heal the sick and preach the gospel, and they show Christianity in operation, in deed as well as in word, in a way more easily understood and perhaps more valued by the careless and the hostile than do any other missionaries. In late years, not in India alone but in China, Persia and many other lands, the Christian women of England and Scotland, of America and Australasia, have set an example to Christian manhood in their numbers, devotion and courage which should provoke men to emulation, and is worthy of the first century. Certainly neither in the first nor in any succeeding century has it ever been surpassed.

Educational work, both higher and lower, is one of the distinguishing features of the Indian mission field. The non-Christian education which is given in Government schools and colleges, though excellent in its own way, has failed to produce any moral improvement among the people. While it has shattered all religious belief among both Hindū and Muḥammadan pupils, it has not attempted to substitute anything in its stead. Conscious of this, the Government has encouraged Hindūs, Muḥammadans and Christians alike to establish schools and colleges of their own. This has been done, but it is only the Christians that have to any adequate extent carried on the work. The importance of getting hold of the youth of the country and training them in all Christian learning cannot be overestimated.

Pastoral and itinerating work is carried on by perhaps every missionary society at work in India. It is of at least as much importance to properly shepherd the congregations already gathered together as to preach the gospel to men as yet unevangelised. In both these departments Indian Christian teachers, catechists

[1] The present writer hopes that the few little works which he has been enabled to produce in Persian may not be devoid of value.

and clergy are extensively employed, just as Indian Christians of both sexes are working in schools, colleges, hospitals and dispensaries, in Zenana visiting and the work of the press, side by side with European and American labourers. The training of Indian workers is largely carried on by many, perhaps by all, of the missionary societies. Theological colleges, for example, exist in connexion with the C.M.S. at Lahore, Ilāhābad, Pūna and other places. It is well understood that foreign missionaries, however high their attainments and however deep their spirituality may be, cannot do more than begin the work of the conversion of India. That grand and glorious task must, under God, be brought to a successful issue by the Indian Church itself. To show to what extent this is generally realised, it may be mentioned that in June 1900 there were working in connexion with one society alone, the C.M.S., 184 native clergy in India, Ceylon and Mauritius, and no fewer than 3541 Indian lay assistants, while the same society had only 313 Europeans, clerical and lay, including lady missionaries but excluding wives, at work in the same field. While the pastoral work is not neglected, itinerating is extensively carried on; and the bands of Associated evangelists are doing good work, which should, however, be largely extended. In quite recent times it has been found possible to open Sunday schools in India for non-Christian children, and good results have already followed.

The hindrances to mission work in India are numerous. Many of them are common to all work for the Master in every part of the world, arising as they do from man's fallen nature. But in India there are those peculiar to the country, notably the opposition of the great ancient religions—Hindūism in India proper, Buddhism in Burma and Ceylon—as well as the more modern religion of Muḥammad in many parts of the country, more especially in the Panjāb, the North-West Provinces, Bengal and Bombay. The institution of Caste has always been a great hindrance to the spread of the Gospel, and it has had its influence not only upon Hindūs, but, it may almost be said, upon Muslims and Europeans too in India. The multiplicity of languages, the degradation of women, and the ignorance of the great mass of the people, have also to be encountered, to say nothing of the deadly nature of the climate and a kind of moral *miasma* which seems to exist in the very air and which the immoralities practised in the name of religion by many Hindū sects favour very extensively. The opposition of the Government may be said to have ceased, and many Europeans in high civil and military positions have by their noble and consistent Christian lives, and often by their generous assistance and encouragement, aided in the Master's work. But in the ranks of irreligious and often ungodly Anglo-Indians there have always been found active opponents of mission work; and such men, both in India and in England, do all in their power to hinder the progress of the Gospel.[1] A distinguished native of India, not himself a Christian, Protap Chunder Mozoomdar, well writes: "The moral force of the Christian religion should not be exhausted by ordained Christian missionaries alone, but every English man and English woman in India should be a messenger of the spirit of their religion. They should be conscious of the great responsibility that rests upon them. The good name and the good influence of the Imperial Government rest upon what each Englishman does and thinks in India. The dense masses of our people have no chance of seeing their honoured Empress, nor have they much chance of knowing the Viceroy who is her representative. But they see and deal with the subordinate officials, and the non-official trader, planter and soldier. If each one of these shaped his conduct according to the laws of life laid down in the New Testament . . . the cause of Indian progress would make greater headway. . . . Perhaps nothing can remove this source of weakness except the sense that each Christian man who goes out to India is a responsible representative of his Queen and his Christ."[2]

The fact that the Indian Government supports the opium trade and issues licences to prostitutes has been again and again cast in the teeth of Christian missionaries in India. It is only by appealing to the conduct of the same Government in refusing to admit the Bible into the educational course in Government schools and colleges, and the proof thereby afforded that the Government of India is *not* a Christian Government, that we can show clearly that Christianity is not responsible for such open scandals and offences to the conscience of every right-

[1] The little book entitled *Are Foreign Missions doing any Good?* published by the C.M.S., contains the opinions expressed in favour of Missions by some of the most distinguished of Anglo-Indian statesmen.

[2] "Present-Day Progress in India," in the *Nineteenth Century* for Dec. 1900.

thinking man, heathen, Muḥammadan, Buddhist and Christian alike.

Modern European infidelity, aided by the abuse of the Higher Criticism (which, *when properly used*, has doubtless something to teach us), has helped to prevent many of the most thoughtful of India's sons from embracing Christianity. Frequently nowadays opponents, instead of endeavouring to defend Hindūism and Muḥammadanism when attacked, employ weapons forged in England and America against Christianity. But even this and all other causes combined do not check the steady onward progress of the Gospel. The Muḥammadans feel this quite as much as the Hindūs, for the Nawāb Mushînu'l Mulk of Ḥaidarābād said some years ago, "To me it seems that as a nation and a religion we are dying out: . . . Unless a miracle of reform occurs, we Muḥammadans are doomed to extinction."[1] No less clearly does Mozoomdar write: "During the last twenty-five years a great change is observable in the attitude of our people towards Christianity. They have certainly great reverence for the life and teachings of Christ; they have largely outgrown the old prejudice against studying the Bible."[2]

The rise of certain great attempts to reform or to revive Hindūism, Islām and Buddhism which the present century has witnessed, such as the Brahmo-Samāj, the Ārya-Samāj, the New Islāmic movement and others similar, shows how Christianity is steadily undermining the foundations upon which these religions rest. Each of them doubtless tends for a time to lessen the number of converts, but the disintegrating effects of these movements is patent, as is their failure to substitute anything which will take the place of the religion of Christ.

A few statistics will show the numerical increase of Christian converts in India in recent years. The report of the Decennial Missionary Conference at the end of 1882 showed that the native Christians in connexion with all Protestant societies amounted to 492,882. This was an increase of 86 per cent. on the numbers ascertained at the meeting of Conference ten years previously,—a rate fifteen times greater than that of the population at large. "The increase in the number of communi-

[1] Quoted by Rev. E. Sell in an article on "The New Islâm" in the *Contemporary Review* for Aug. 1893.

[2] *Nineteenth Century*, Dec. 1900.

cants was yet more striking, being at the rate of 114 per cent. in the ten years."[1] When the census for 1891 was taken, it was found that the Protestant Indian Christians numbered 648,843. The census for 1901 will probably show that they number not far short of one million. There were in all, including Syrian Jacobites and all other Syrians and the Roman Catholics, as nearly as possible 2,036,000 native Christians in India in 1891.[2] The number seems comparatively a large one; but when we remember that the total population of India in that year amounted to 287,223,431, we see that the Christians are hardly to be noticed, numerically speaking. There is, therefore, an immense work still to be done, for *the yearly increase of Hindūs and Muḥammadans by births alone adds far more to their numbers than are yet won over to Christianity in any one year.*[3] Yet in connexion with one single missionary society, the C.M.S., no fewer than 8919 baptisms took place in India, Ceylon and Mauritius in the year ending 1st June 1900. These include the baptisms of the children of converts; but not many years ago those converts in many cases—their grandparents in perhaps all—were themselves heathen or Muslims.

Yet the Protestant missionaries societies are agreed in seeking *quality* not *quantity*. In other words, while preaching the truth as it is in Jesus to all whom they can possibly reach, they do not baptize anyone hastily, but first endeavour to assure themselves not only of his religious knowledge, but of his true and living faith in the Saviour. Of course, in the Indian Church at the present day, just as in that at Corinth in St. Paul's time, unworthy members are to be found. But are not such to be discovered nearer home? In spite of all hindrances and drawbacks, the work is succeeding; and the Christian Churches of the present day are, by God's blessing, effecting the object aimed at even in the first century but never yet accomplished—that of the conversion of India to the Christian faith.

Before concluding this brief and imperfect sketch of mission work in India, we must refer to two great dangers which threaten the native Christian community there, and which, if not firmly resisted in the power of God's Holy Spirit, may do much to mar the work of God in that land.

[1] *Hist. of the C.M.S.*, by Mr. Eugene Stock, vol. iii. p. 143.

[2] Taken from "Indian Government Census," *loc. cit.* pp. 509, 510.

[3] The population is shown by the census of 1901 to amount to 294,266,701.

There is great danger of our transplanting to and perpetuating in India the "unhappy divisions" which have for various reasons, though doubtless overruled for good, done so much to keep Christ's followers from uniting with one another in the bonds of love at home. All true Christians *are* one in Christ, members of the one Catholic or Universal Church. Yet we all know how ignorance and prejudice have begotten sectarian feeling, leading one body of Protestants to hold aloof from others, the Church of England, for example, from the Wesleyans, who were driven forth from that Church in the days of her deadness. Although the differences in Church government which distinguish the Church of England from the Church of Scotland and the other Presbyterian branches of the Church are due more to "accident" or incidents in past history than to anything else, yet many Christians of both communities fail to see this. Men who have "one Lord, one Faith, one Baptism, one God and Father of all," and who believe in, love, and serve the one Saviour, may surely agree to differ on minor points, and acknowledge that, as monarchy may be better suited to one land and republicanism to another, or to a different period, so different methods of Church government may alike be of Divine appointment. Work in the mission-field and the guidance of the Holy Spirit have taught many missionaries to realise this better than some Christians at home do. Christian converts in India realise their unity with one another, though they have been brought out of darkness to the light, humanly speaking, by varied instrumentality. There can then be no advantage gained by endeavouring to accentuate the minor differences between Protestant Christians in such a way as to divide the Indian Christian Church for all time into Episcopalian, Wesleyan, Presbyterian, Baptist and other parties. Yet it is difficult to see how this rending of the fair robe of Christ, this preaching and propagation of schism, can be avoided, unless those at home who direct mission work abroad realise the danger and strive to avoid it ere it is too late. We should work and pray for the establishment of a great indigenous Evangelical Church in India, holding fast the essentials of the faith, yet as wide as Bible Christianity itself. Whoever endeavours to perpetuate in India the divisions of Western Christendom is, however great his zeal and however good his motives may be, doing his best to hinder the accomplishment of the desire expressed by our Lord in His prayer before His death on the Cross for us all, "That they all may be One."

The second great danger is that of the growth of heresy, and more especially of that sacerdotal heresy which has corrupted the simplicity of the Gospel in the Church of Rome, the Eastern Church and in all that remains of the ancient Churches of Asia. It is well known how the essentially false and un-Christian sacerdotal system has of late years infected other branches of Christ's Church also. History shows that this is the gangrene from which Churches die. There is great danger even now in India, lest, in bringing a convert into communion with certain Churches, we should be bringing him under the influence of a delusion which, as history plainly shows us, tends to separate men from Christ by putting mere human beings between them and their God. There is danger that a Muḥammadan convert, who has at least always held to the truth that idolatry is a deadly sin, should learn to bow down to "Christian idols,"—to adore a piece of bread! It would be a poor result of all the labour undertaken in India for the spread of the Gospel, to see the people of that land, though nominally Christian, as far from Christ as are the inhabitants of Italy or Spain. If that should ever come about—which God in His mercy forbid—it will be caused by such false teaching.

Finally, if the work of the conversion of India is to be accomplished, more workers are needed in every department and in every part of the country. These, being picked men in every sense, and, above all, filled with the Spirit, should be carefully and systematically trained *at home*, in some measure, before they go out to encounter the dangers to health which, in so many cases, shorten the work of the missionary in India. The soldier of Christ should go out armed and equipped with at least some rudimentary knowledge of *one* of the languages in which he has to preach the Gospel, and with some elementary but correct acquaintance with the main tenets of at least one of the religions of the country. This wise plan was in its early days adopted by the Church Missionary Society.[1] It is to be regretted that it was ever abandoned by them.

[1] *Hist. of the C.M.S.* vol. i. p. 266: "The languages of the mission-field were then regarded as an important part of the studies" (at Islington College), "and three months later another important examination took place of the Oriental classes conducted by Professor S. Lee in Hebrew, Arabic, Sanskrit and Bengali."

Shall not we Christians of Britain and America, in this the beginning of a new Christian century, hearken to the Master speaking to us to-day far more clearly than even to His first disciples, and saying to us as He said to them nearly nineteen centuries ago—

"The harvest truly is plenteous, but the labourers are few; pray ye, therefore, the Lord of the Harvest, that He will send forth"—thrust forth—"labourers into His Harvest."

NOTE.—As the census returns for 1901 are not yet published, we quote the following passage from the *Dnyanodaya*, which shows, on the authority of the *Indian Christian Directory* of 1900, the estimate then formed of the Indian Christian population, omitting that of Further India:—"The Protestant Indian community is said to number 772,055. There are 1010 Protestant Indian Christian ordained ministers, 590 medical men, 1098 in Government service on incomes of over Rs.50 per month, 92 lawyers, 15 civil engineers. 39,060 Indian Christians are returned as supporting themselves by agriculture. This will surprise many. About 33,000 Christians out of 772,055, *i.e.* about one twenty-fourth of the whole, are in some way connected with Missions as agents. 391,166 children are reported to be in mission schools, or in some way connected with the Christian community. In a few years these youths will be adult members of the community. The Protestant Indian Christians of Ceylon are put at 55,193."

CHAPTER V[1]

A MISSIONARY'S PROPER ATTITUDE TOWARDS NON-CHRISTIAN RELIGIONS AND PHILOSOPHIES.

THERE is good reason to believe that many persons, otherwise well informed, cherish serious misconceptions with reference to missionary work. One of the most common of these is the view which they entertain regarding the attitude adopted by the Christian missionary, and the Missionary Society to which he belongs, towards the different religions and great philosophies with which he is brought in contact. Many persons consider that we take up a quite unjustifiable position in this respect; and this misconception causes us to lose the help and sympathy of many thoughtful and earnest men, who, if they knew what our attitude really is, might very materially aid us in accomplishing the noblest task ever intrusted to mortal men, since their own reason and calm judgment would show them that we are engaged in the discharge of a distinct duty, to shirk which would be conduct unworthy of Christian Englishmen. The aim of the present chapter is to define our position, and at the same time to show that it is logical, justifiable and necessary, under all the circumstances of the case.

Many people credit missionaries with a firm conviction that all religions but the Christian are simply and solely devices of the Evil One intended to destroy men's souls. They believe that we, acting under this conviction, consider ourselves obliged to oppose all such religions at every point and in every possible manner, and to do our best to do away with them entirely. On the other hand, owing to our increased acquaintance with the great religions and philosophies of the

[1] This and the following chapter in a slightly different form originally appeared in the *Church Missionary Intelligencer*.

East, people are learning the fact that in every such faith or system there is to be found a certain modicum of truth and wisdom. The amount of these qualities which may exist in any such religion is very frequently exaggerated, because of that "little knowledge" which is so proverbially dangerous. Owing to the immense multiplication of sciolists in our own day and generation, and to the too frequent rejection of the inductive method of reasoning from facts in favour of the (to certain minds) more fascinating if less logical method of formulating hasty and startling theories, and then by some Procrustean system forcing the actual facts of the case into seeming conformity with them,—which intellectual pastime is very popular at present,—such mistakes frequently occur. A superficial student of Comparative Religion is only too apt to content himself with hasty generalisations, and to mistake, for example, the Hindū *Tṛimûrtti* for the Christian doctrine of the Trinity, or the Indian theory of Yôga for the Christian's yearning for union with God, or again the Buddhist Nirvâṇa for the "life and incorruption"[1] brought to light by Christ Jesus. It is only by a careful and long continued study of the "Ethnic Scriptures" in their original languages that one can possibly in any degree enter into the mind and thought of those who composed them, and thus be able to understand at all correctly what their teachings signify to those who cherish such books as enshrining the doctrines of their ancestral faith. It is the want of such thoroughly accurate and scientific study, coupled as it too frequently is with an eager desire for novelty and a false liberality of sentiment (similar to that of a certain, now disgraced, literary man, who professed his inability to recognise any distinction between the moral and the immoral, but recognised only the "artistic" and the "inartistic"), that leads many otherwise logical minds to imagine that Christianity differs in *degree* merely and not in *kind* from other great systems of religion. Of course persons who assume the latter theory as an *axiom* and refuse to argue about it will never be able—until they receive something far higher than any merely intellectual enlightenment—to enter at all into the objects and aims of a Christian missionary, whether he belongs to the first or to the twentieth century. Our present appeal and ἀπολογία is, however, addressed not to them, but to more thoughtful men.

[1] 2 Tim. i. 10.

When one has carefully and honestly studied other great systems of religion and philosophy, ancient as well as modern, one finds that his first hopeful impressions of the amount of truth inculcated in these systems were far more favourable to them than a rigorous examination of them has justified. Yet the student most undoubtedly concludes, as Augustine remarked so many centuries ago, that some degree of truth may be found to underlie every such religion or philosophy. This being the case, men feel that to condemn all non-Christian religions and philosophies as entirely false and destitute of the slightest modicum of truth, or even of any sign of a yearning after God, would be unjust and unworthy of a Christian. Yet this is precisely what they fancy that the ordinary Christian missionary not only does, but is by his very profession obliged to do. Nothing, our critics tell us, can do more harm, and prove a greater obstacle to the progress of civilisation and enlightenment and the growth of friendly feeling between the great nations of the East and ourselves, than to make a practice of denouncing the doctrines which non-Christians have held from their own childhood, and perhaps from the very origin of their national existence, as alike evil and absurd. This must be especially the case, we are assured, when those who have been well trained in the tenets of their ancestral faith, and who have in their possession sacred books of great antiquity, stored in some cases at least with the best and deepest wisdom and the loftiest thoughts of many of the greatest teachers of ancient times, are suddenly called upon to cast them all aside as not only worthless but positively injurious,—and that, too, by men who have not taken the trouble, or have not perhaps the learning and ability requisite, to enable them to study these ancient and hallowed writings. And therefore, we are told, it is folly, and worse than folly, for us to send missionaries to China where the people have grown wise and tender-hearted under the tuition of Confucius and Mencius; or to endeavour to lead astray from the lofty philosophy of Buddha the people of Ceylon, of Japan, or of Thibet. Or again, it is perfectly hopeless for us to endeavour to convert the Muḥammadan world, we are assured, while we persist in denouncing Muḥammad as a false prophet, and while we fail to recognise that (as a late dignitary of the Church of England told us not very long ago) Muḥammadanism forms high and noble characters. Nor can we hope for better success with the Hindūs, our critics admonish us, if we ignorantly believe and assert that the Hindū faith is degrading and immoral. Our readers will remember that remarks and criticisms of this kind have been most plentifully showered upon us in recent works, principally composed by members of the noble army of globe-trotters, regarding whom, if there be one thing more certain than another, it is that, however great their attainments in other respects may be, *they* have *not* devoted to the study of the much-praised Oriental religions and philosophies in their original languages one-hundredth part of the time and attention necessary to qualify them to entertain and to express any opinion whatever on the subject. Whether or not they are right in accusing missionaries of neglecting to study these great systems, it is certain that our critics themselves are, generally speaking, guilty of the very offence with which they charge us, as at once becomes apparent from even a cursory perusal of their works.

On the other hand, it may surprise some of those who, on such grounds as those above referred to, object to the work of all missionary societies, to learn that we missionaries sometimes find it very hard to realise that there still, even at the beginning of the twentieth century, exists among Christian people in Britain such a total lack of acquaintance with our position and methods of work as to make it possible for them to fancy that we really assume towards non-Christian religions and philosophies in general such an attitude as they attribute to us. Let us discuss the matter on *à priori* grounds. Presumably people know that missionaries, comprising among their number many men of university training, cannot *all* be completely and blissfully ignorant of *classical* learning at least. Now how is it possible, let us ask, for a man who has even a slight acquaintance with the classical masterpieces of the literature of ancient Greece and Rome, who has entered into the spirit of the classical poets and philosophers, who has stood with Socrates before his judges, or with Æschylus has pondered the deep problems of human life, to be entirely devoid of sympathy with such men as these? Can anyone read Homer and not agree with the aged Nestor's son in holding that in all men there exists a thirst[1] for the knowledge of God? Or, again, can he doubt that Pindar's voicing

[1] Πάντες δὲ θεῶν χατέουσ' ἄνθρωποι, *Odyss.* iii. 48.

forth of the old tradition of the Elysian fields,[1] where some hereafter

> *ἄδακρυν νέμονται*
> *αἰῶνα,*

was the expression of a truth in some manner learnt from God[2] Himself? If we acknowledge that, among the nations of classical antiquity, God did not leave Himself without witness,[3] how can we be justly accused of denying something of the same Divine guidance to men of other and even more ancient nations also? Surely we may fairly expect to be given credit for candour enough to confess that, just as in the writings of Plato and Epictetus, of Aristotle and Marcus Antoninus, of Cicero and even Lucretius, many noble sentiments and much truth[4] may be found which we could ill afford to lack, so also in the Ṛig-Veda of India, and still more in the Bhagavadgîtâ and similar works, nay even in such epics and tales as the Mahâbhârata and Śakuntalâ, we may meet with not a few noble ideas, and with much that is worthy of careful study and attention. What is true of Indian literature is true likewise of the Eddas of Scandinavia,[5] of the legends of

[1] Pindar, *Olymp.* ii. vers. 61–77: *Ἶσον δὲ νύκτεσσιν αἰεί*, etc. Cf. Homer, *Odyss.* iv. 563–568.

[2] *Πᾶσα δόσις ἀγαθὴ καὶ πᾶν δώρημα τέλειον ἄνωθέν ἐστι, καταβαῖνον ἀπὸ τοῦ Πατρὸς τῶν φώτων*, Jas. i. 17.

[3] *Οὐκ ἀμάρτυρον ἑαυτὸν ἀφῆκεν*, Acts xiv. 17.

[4] The scattered elements of truth that may be found among non-Christian systems are in a large measure the remains of a primitive Revelation (*pace* Professor Max Müller); and in this respect they may be compared to the shattered fragments of a noble picture or of a broken mirror once intended to reflect the image of God, but which no amount of human ingenuity ever sufficed to piece together until the new Revelation of God in Christ enabled men, however faintly, to see what connection these scattered fragments originally had with one another, and what they were intended to represent. Yet we may add with Bede, "In quantum vero vel gustum aliquem sapientiae cuiuslibet vel virtutis imaginem habebant, totum hoc desuper acceperunt, *non solum* munere primae conditionis, verum etiam *quotidiana Eius gratia*, Qui creaturam Suam nec Se deserentem deserens, dona Sua, prout Ipse indicaverit hominibus et magna magnis et parva largitur parvis" (Bede, *Exposit. in Cant. Cantt.*, *Opp.* ix. 197, ed. Giles).

[5] For example, in the *Edda Saemundar Hinns Fróða*, Vǫluspá, stanzas 61 and 66, we read (Hildebrand's ed. pp. 16, 17)—

"Sér hon upp koma	She (the Prophetess) sees arise
ǫðru sinni	A second time
iǫrð or oegi	Earth from ocean

Assyria and Babylonia, of some of the philosophical thoughts of ancient Egyptian sages,[1] of the Zend Avesta, of Arabian poets and traditionalists, and even of the Qur'ân itself. We do not merely say that missionaries *should* recognise such facts as these, because they are true. What our own experience enables us to affirm is that *these facts are and have long been recognised by all missionaries of any mark.* Our position is precisely analogous in this respect to that of the great Apostle of the Gentiles. As he once appealed to an altar erected in honour of the Unknown God,[2] and on another occasion quoted the assertion of a heathen poet[3] that men are in a certain sense the children of God, and pointed out that these expressed great truths, the full significance of which his hearers needed to have *more* deeply impressed upon their hearts and consciences,—so we also believe and know that it is possible to draw from their own literature and traditions lessons which the non-Christian nations of to-day need (not to cast aside and forget, but on the contrary) to learn and treasure up and ponder in their inmost hearts and souls. We, who are followers of Him who declared Himself to be the Truth, feel that for His sake we must welcome truth wherever we may find it, and that, too, not grudgingly or of necessity, but gladly and cordially. Nay more, we consider any such truth accepted by any nation or sect to be a step in advance upon the road to God.

But, on the other hand, we find ourselves compelled by our regard for truth and honesty not to confine ourselves to a merely *superficial* acquaintance with the various non-Christian

iðjagroena :	Beauteously green :
. . . .	. . . . . .
. . . .	. . . . . .
Sal sér hon standa	She sees stand a hall
sólu fegra,	Fairer than the Sun,
gulli þaktan	Covered with gold
á Gimlé.	In Heaven.
þar skulu dyggvar	There shall righteous
dróttir byggja	Peoples dwell
ok um aldrdaga	And for eternity
yndis nióta.	Happiness enjoy."

[1] *E.g.* "Ar reθ sen n nuter," "Man is the image (*or* comrade) of God"; quoted in P. Pierret's *Vocabulaire Hiéroglyphique*, p. 499.

[2] Acts xvii. 23.

[3] Acts xvii. 28, Τοῦ γὰρ καὶ γένος ἐσμέν, Cleanthes, Hymn: in Jov. 8; Aratus, Phaenomena.

religions and philosophies with which our work in its various departments brings us into contact. A missionary labouring among Buddhists, for example, would hardly be deemed adequately equipped for his work if he were to content himself, in studying that great and interesting system of thought, with a perusal of Arnold's *Light of Asia*, as the publishers[1] of that able poem (which can hardly claim to be regarded as a critical *exposé* of Buddhism) inform us that many "English Buddhists" do! Nor should we consider that a knowledge of Professor Max Müller's clever and interesting, though rather imaginative and romantic, "Hibbert Lectures" for 1878 would qualify a missionary to contend with or even to understand the true nature of Hinduism, either past or present. As well accept Carlyle or Davenport or Canon Isaac Taylor as exponents of Islâm![2] Our duty alike to our Divine Master, who has sent us forth as His witnesses, and to those for whose conversion we go, forbids us to indulge in this solemn trifling with deep and terrible facts. In order even to qualify ourselves in the eyes of our societies for missionary work in the field, we are obliged to study the religions of the people among whom we labour. We are not content to learn merely what it was that their ancestors believed a few thousand years ago; we must also know what their priests now inculcate and what the people believe and practise. We do not feel satisfied when we cull from their sacred books a few nobly-sounding precepts, and, separating these from their context it may be, give them an application and a depth of meaning of which their writers never dreamt, and which the modern professors of these religions repudiate. But, while making all due allowance for aught of truth or wisdom we may find, while thanking God for this and employing it to bring men back to Him, we do not and cannot close our eyes to the falsehood and the evil, the immorality and the ignorance, with which this modicum of truth and wisdom is too often overlaid or perverted. Reason, truth, justice, duty, humanity and Christian charity alike forbid this. The most impartial critics admit the fact that the religions and philosophies of Greece and Rome were impotent, or worse than impotent, from a moral point of

[1] See Trübner's ed., Pref.

[2] Except, of course, that while these latter writers on Islâm knew (apparently) nothing of Arabic, Sir Edwin Arnold and Professor Max Müller are noted as masters of Sanskṛit.

view.[1] They acknowledge that all the lofty systems of Greek philosophy ended in Pyrrhonism or universal doubt. Their admiration for Socrates, for Plato, for Aristotle, does not lead them to deny the deep uncertainty on the highest of all themes under which these great men laboured, nor to conceal the fact that they felt, to use Plato's own expression, the need of some "Divine Word"[2] to bear them over the sea of Life. Nor does the student of the Classics deny the vileness of Martial and Catullus, or question the truth of the fearful picture of the abysmal depth of abomination into which society had sunk, as depicted for us not more clearly in the first chapter of the Epistle to the Romans than in Juvenal, Tacitus, Suetonius and the poets mentioned above. Hardly anyone with any pretence to being a Christian will venture to assert that Greece and Rome had no need for the Gospel of Christ, or that the Saviour of the world made a mistake in sending His disciples to them, or even in coming into the world at the enlightened and civilised epoch of Roman history in which He appeared. *Yet precisely this position is taken up (in practice if not in theory) by many professing Christians of to-day* with reference to modern non-Christian nations, in spite of the fact that, from the point of view of immorality and of religious uncertainty at least, many heathen and Muḥammadan nations of our own time are in quite as miserable a condition as were Greece and Rome in the days of St. Paul.

In acting thus, we hold, the critics and opponents of missionary work are not true to their own principles. We ourselves, on the other hand, refusing to be led astray from the path of duty and of obedience to our Master's parting command by the false liberality of the day,—which springs as much from ignorance as from unwillingness to obey that command,—find that the half-truths and the noble aspirations of the non-Christian world after better things plead with us not less touchingly than do its falsehoods and its crimes, its doubts and its despair, for the light of the glorious Gospel of Christ.

We are often accused of drawing too dark a picture of the

[1] The writer of the work entitled Ἔρωτες, ascribed to Lucian, says, *Αἱ δὲ ποίκιλαι σοφίαι . . . μόλις . . . εἰς τ' οὐμφανὲς ἔμελλον ἥξειν, ἵνα τῇ θείᾳ φιλοσοφίᾳ καὶ τὸ παιδεραστεῖν συνακμάσῃ*, Sec. 35.

[2] *Εἰ μή τις δύναιτο ἀσφαλέστερον καὶ ἀκινδυνότερον ἐπὶ βεβαιοτέρου ὀχήματος ἢ λόγου θείου τινὸς διαπορευθῆναι*, *Phaedo*, xxxv.

moral state of the non-Christian world, and of the evil effects which many of these religions exercise upon the lives of their professors. The truth is that there is hardly one of us in the mission-field that does not feel that shame seals his lips and restrains his pen whenever he wishes to give Christian people at home any idea, however faint, of the actual state of affairs in heathen and Muḥammadan lands. How can we venture, for instance, to explain what the leading religious symbols of India at the present day — the *linga* and the *yôni* — really mean? Or again, how can we give people any adequate conception of what is really implied in the infant marriages of both Hindūs and Muslims, in the temporary marriages permitted by the Shî'eh religious law and practised in some Sunnî communities too, in the Muḥammadan systems of divorce and concubinage, to say nothing of even infinitely *worse* evils? If we *could*, perhaps people would be startled out of the fool's paradise in which so many now ensconce themselves, and which such illustrations of Muḥammadan tenderness of heart and liberality of sentiment as hapless Armenia a few years ago afforded do not suffice to make them abandon.

But while our own knowledge and experience of various non-Christian systems suffice to make us conscious of some at least of the unspeakable evils *sanctioned* by one or other of these religions, — slavery, child-marriages, and wars for the spread of Islâm are directly sanctioned by Muḥammadanism,— it is utterly erroneous to impute to us the belief that *all* Hindūs and Muslims and all other non-Christians alike are totally given over to vices of the vilest kind, and are therefore quite destitute of generosity, purity, and of every noble aspiration. We missionaries know better than that. No one of us would venture to deny that among professed heathen and Muslims there are to be found not a few who are brave, generous, noble-minded, and in some cases true, honest, and perhaps even pure. Such men, we believe, are as surely to be found in Muḥammadan and heathen lands to-day as in ancient times their prototypes existed in Greece and Rome. Are there none such in China, in Japan, in Africa? Surely Zoroaster, Buddha, Confucius were men of this type. We hold with thankfulness to the conviction that God has not even now left Himself without a witness in Muḥammadan and heathen hearts. Tertullian's well-known statement that the soul of man is "naturally Christian"[1] and bears witness to its Creator, is fully borne out by our own experience. Were it not that we firmly believe this, and feel confident that, amid the teeming millions of the non-Christian world, there are multitudes of men and women who long for a knowledge of the true God, and who, in spite of the surrounding darkness, are striving to walk by every little ray of light which conscience or intuition or tradition may still preserve for them, our hearts would sometimes fail us in doing our God-appointed work. But, though we hope and believe that even heathenism and Muḥammadanism have not in every case entirely quenched the "Light that lighteth every man coming into the world,"[2] yet we have too much knowledge of these systems to be deluded into fancying that such noble traits or high-toned characters have been *formed* by Islâm or by any other such creed. As well hold up Socrates or Plato as products of the teachings of the mythologists, whom the latter philosopher excluded from his ideal Republic because of their *immoral* influence. Some men are better, some worse than their creed.

"The world by wisdom knew not God."[3] No truer word than this can be found in Holy Writ. As this is true of the Greek and Roman world of ancient times, its own philosophers and sages being witnesses, it is true also of ancient India and China, of ancient Egypt and Babylonia, and of modern Arabia and Persia as well. Only One has ever said—only One could say truly—"I am the Way, the Truth, and the Life; no man cometh unto the Father but by Me."[4] To refuse to heathen and Muḥammadan nations the knowledge of Him who rightly claimed to be the "Light of the World,"[5] on the plea that their own religions are sufficient or are even best for them, would be as cruel and would display as much utter ignorance of the facts of the case as it would were we to contend that the old medical system of Galen and Hippocrates, still practised in the East, is best for Orientals, and that it is but bigotry to introduce among them our present systems of medicine and surgery. With regard to medicine no one would venture to make such an absurd statement; but with regard to the infinitely more important matter of religion it is by some considered as a sign

[1] "O testimonium animae naturaliter Christianae!" (Tert. *Liber Apologet.* cap. xvii.)

[2] John i. 9.

[3] 1 Cor. i. 21.

[4] John xiv. 6.

[5] John viii. 12.

of great liberality of mind to argue thus, and of narrowness and intolerance to act in a rational manner and according to our Lord's express command.

Would that all those who honestly differ from us in this matter would carefully and diligently study the nature of the various religions already referred to, and the state of the countries where they still hold sway. Would that the influence of Muḥammadanism, for instance, as shown in the history of India, of Arabia, of North Africa, of Turkey, of Persia, for the last thousand years were impartially studied. Then, perhaps, earnest men's hearts would be stirred within them, and they would, as philanthropists, as Christians, as *men*, long to bring to those who still sit in darkness the good news that the Light of the Divine Word, for which Socrates and Plato yearned, for which among the heathen and Muslims of our own day countless noble souls are yearning, and which all need, though perchance they know it not, has indeed shone forth from the Glory of God in the face of Jesus Christ.

CHAPTER VI

THE CHRISTIANITY WHICH INDIA NEEDS.

"Those wise answers of the far-off sage,
So wise, they shut out God, and can enchain
To-day in narrow bonds of foolishness
The subtle Eastern brain."

—L. MORRIS, "The Wanderer."

"L'idéal chrétien est devant nous depuis dix-huit siécles ; il brille de notre temps avec une telle intensité qu'il faut faire de grands efforts pour ne pas voir que tous nos maux proviennent de ce que nous ne le prenons pas pour guide. Mais plus il devient difficile de ne pas le voir, plus certains hommes augmentent d'efforts pour nous persuader de faire comme eux, de fermer les yeux afin de ne pas le voir. Pour être bien sûr d'arriver, il faut surtout jeter la boussole par-dessus bord—disent-ils—et ne point s'arrêter."—TOLSTOI.

IN one of an interesting series of articles upon some of the chief leaders of thought in India during the nineteenth century, which the late Professor Max Müller a few years ago contributed to *Cosmopolis*, that eminent Sanskṛitist, in speaking of Keshub Chunder Sen and his followers, writes thus :—

"There were no Christian ambassadors to grasp the hand that was stretched out. Such missionaries as were in India then wanted unconditional submission, not *union or conciliation*. They were themselves fettered by superstitions which men of the type of Rammohun Roy had long discarded. . . . The philosophy of the Vedânta . . . remained . . . the firm foundation of their religion. . . . When he was in England it was doubtful whether he, in his mind, a Vedântist, was not in his heart a Christian. . . . We shall see that some of his followers surrendered even that outward badge of Brâhmaṇism" (the sacred thread), "but they could not surrender that ineradicable belief in the substantial identity of the eternal element in God and man. A man like Athanasius might easily have brought them to call it the divine sonship of man, if that expression had been fully explained to them. But no one was there, nay, no one seems even now bold enough to speak out, and to separate the vital kernel from the perishable crust of religion. That vital kernel was more clearly seen by Rammohun Roy than by many of the missionaries who came to enlighten him. In Rammohun Roy's translation of the Upanishads we can clearly see that in his views of the Deity and of the relation between the human and the Divine, he had never yielded an inch of his old Hindū convictions, though his practical religion was saturated with Christian sentiments."[1]

It seems at first sight rather curious to find "Athanasius contra mundum," who so nobly contended against the Arian attempt to detract from the essential Deity of Christ, held up as an example to Christian missionaries to show them the wisdom of *modifying the Gospel* in order to commend it to the Hindū mind. But passing over this and the question of what is meant by the "eternal element in God," we turn to the consideration of a more important matter,—one that is directly or indirectly referred to, not only in the article already quoted, but in very many of the periodicals and even in much of the light literature of the present day,—the desirability or otherwise of so altering and improving (?) the Christian Faith as to render it acceptable in its modified form to those who will not accept it as it is.

If we understand Professor Max Müller's contention aright, he held that what is needed at the present time in India is the formation of some eclectic system of Theosophy (in the proper meaning of that much-abused term), which, by blending the esoteric teaching of Christianity (apart from its doctrinal system) with the speculations of Hindū philosophers, will satisfy the aspirations and longings of thoughtful and earnest Hindūs. That we are not misrepresenting the Professor's meaning is clear from the fact that he informs us that he himself advised Keshub Chunder Sen to have the New Testament translated into Sanskṛit, and into some of the leading Indian vernaculars for the instruction of his fellow-countrymen, *only leaving out the historical passages and any other chapters or verses which he considered inappropriate for influencing the Indian mind.*[2] The opinion thus expressed as to the possibility and the desirability of such a fusion of Hindū and Christian teaching is one which, as we have said, is in some form or other very prevalent, not only among earnest students of Comparative Religion, but also among that large class of people who, as Thucy-

[1] "My Indian Friends" (*Cosmopolis* for August 1898, pp. 340, 341).

[2] *Cosmopolis* for August 1898, p. 348.

dides says,[1] finding the search for truth so difficult, turn to whatever lies nearest at hand and seems most generally accepted in the circle to which they belong. People fancy that it is narrow-minded to conceive of Christianity as the Absolute Religion, and prefer to believe that it is possible to construct some new creed which will contain within itself all that is true and noble in all existing faiths, and will thus form a religion acceptable to all men alike. To this new religion not only Islâm and Christianity, but also Brâhmaṇism,[2] Buddhism, and all other faiths and philosophies, ancient and modern, are to contribute, though not perhaps in equal measure. All that is dogmatical, historical, local, in every one of the existing religions is to be abolished, and mankind are to become brothers in faith, and never again to contend with one another about such outgrown fallacies as particular doctrines and systems of theology. The object of the present chapter is to inquire to what extent such an amalgamation of Christianity with other faiths is possible and desirable.

Is it possible or desirable to form a Christo-Brâhmaṇical religio-philosophical system which would take the place of all the varied and mutually contradictory creeds that at present obtain in India, and which would be more readily accepted by the people, and would be better adapted to their requirements than the simple and unaltered Gospel of Christ? In the same way, should we hope to construct in Japan, Ceylon and China a philosophy, or a system of Theosophy, which would enable earnest and thoughtful Buddhists, without cutting themselves adrift from the ideas and customs of their fathers, to unite with cultured Europeans in one enlightened and all-embracing creed? Is there no common ground on which Christians and Muslims may unite in worship? Or should we not strive to bind all the nations of the world together in a true and real Religion of the Human Race, in which all men, sinking all differences, and eliminating all that is distinctive in their various beliefs, may unite as members of one great family, of one Universal Church?

It must be confessed that to the human intellect there is something alluring in such a suggestion. We now know that truth lies at the root of all that is erroneous, and that some-

[1] Οὕτως ἀταλαίπωρος τοῖς πολλοῖς ἡ ζήτησις τῆς ἀληθείας, καὶ ἐπὶ τὰ ἑτοῖμα μᾶλλον τρέπονται, Thucydides, i. 20.

[2] Cf. Max Müller's *Hibbert Lectures* for 1878, pp. 377, 378.

thing good and worthy of careful and even reverent consideration may be found not only in every system of philosophy, but still more in every religion. We, as Christians, believe that God has never left Himself without a witness in the hearts of His creatures, and we hold that, "if we will but listen attentively, we can hear in all religions a groaning of the spirit, a struggle to conceive the inconceivable, to utter the unutterable, a longing after the Infinite, a love of God."[1] We know that "God fulfils Himself in many ways." We are aware that Judaism, though one of the Divine methods of preparing the way of Christ, was not the only method used by the Creator for the furtherance of His purpose of redemption. Christ was not only the "end of the law," but the end and aim to which all Greek and Roman, all Hindū and Chinese, philosophy also tended, however unconsciously. If Plato and Aristotle, Pythagoras, and even Pyrrho, in Europe, prepared the way for the reception of the Gospel, how can we venture to deny that in India, Patanjali and Vyâsa, Buddha and Kapila, Kaṇâda, and the unknown author of the Bhagavadgîtâ, nay, even the materialistic Çârvâka himself (the Epicurus of India), had their part in the Divine scheme which brings good out of things evil?[2] But it is one thing to admit this, and quite another thing to fancy that an eclectic system of religion can be constructed, to which Christianity and these various religions and philosophies shall all on an equal footing contribute. We are told of a Roman emperor who wished to admit Christ into the classical Pantheon, and give Him a place with Orpheus, or even with Venus, among the deities of the Imperial City; but the success of this ingenious plan was not such as to encourage us to repeat it. Nor do we believe that, were such a fusion of Christianity with other systems possible, the newly-coined religion would in any degree satisfy the needs of a single human being. We may learn much from Plato, much from Buddha, much from Maulânâ-yi-Rûm. But the most important lesson which they and all other philosophers teach us is, that no philosophy can satisfy the soul of man made in the image of God. Well does Fronto,[3] in speaking of the "Consolations" of Seneca, remark that all such human reasonings cannot heal the broken heart of a parent mourning over

[1] Max Müller, *Hibbert Lectures*, 1878, p. 23.
[2] Cf. Pseudo-Dionysius Areopagita, *De Div. Nom.* iv. 30.
[3] "De Nepote Amisso."

the grave of his lost child. We do not need a Pyrrho to teach us the vanity in this respect of all human philosophy, for even Plato himself, as we have already seen, compares the best and most irrefragable of all such speculations to a raft, upon which, only in default of some firmer vessel, such as some word of God, would the storm-tossed mariner strive to cross the ocean of existence.[1] And, to refer to the myth which Plato uses here as an illustration, it is only when his raft is dashed in pieces on the rocky shore, that at last, by the aid of a Divine person, the shipwrecked Ulysses is enabled to land in safety.[2] All history and experience teach us that, as of old in the storm on the Sea of Galilee, there is only *one* Voice which can bid the billows rest, and say to the human soul, "It is I: be not afraid."

Everyone who has studied Indian philosophy, however slightly, is aware that the six recognised systems as taught in that country, though differing from one another very materially—as is the manner of philosophies in Europe also, both in ancient and in modern times—yet have certain great characteristics in common. Indian philosophy is even more crudely materialistic than Greek, and the *prakṛiti* plays in Indian writings perhaps even a more important part than the ὕλη in Hellenic speculations.[3] As in Greece, so in India, philosophy has ever been in danger, if it endeavoured to escape from Dualism, of ending in a blind Pantheism not far removed from Atheism. Indian aphorisms about the *paramâtman* and the *jîvâtman* can hardly be said to lead the inquirer as far as Plato and Aristotle led their disciples in the search for God; and we know that Plato, in the *Timaeus*, acknowledged how difficult it is to discover the Creator and Father of the Universe, and how impossible to describe Him to the multitude.[4] The early creed of the Vedântists, "There is only one Thing in existence, and no second,"[5] has now practically become the axiomatic foundation of modern philosophy in India, and leaves no room for a Creator. We all know something of the influence which the belief in the illusory nature (*mâyâ*) of all things cognisable to the senses still exerts over the Hindū mind, and

[1] *Phaedo*, 85 D.

[2] *Odyss.* v. *fin.*

[3] Aristotle affirms that the dogma Οὐδὲν γίνεται ἐκ τοῦ μὴ ὄντος was generally held (περὶ γὰρ ταύτης ὁμογνωμονοῦσι τῆς δόξης ἅπαντες οἱ περὶ φύσεως).

[4] *Timaeus*, 10.

[5] "*Êkam êvâdvitîyam.*"

we are aware that the doctrine of metempsychosis is regarded as needing no argument to prove it. It is only quite recently that an able Indian writer, in criticising Mr. Balfour's *Foundations of Belief*, stated that his fellow-countrymen had never yet been able to affirm the existence in Divine Nature of any preference for the good and any hatred of evil. This testimony is true. How, then, is it possible to conceive of any religious system being devised in which Indian philosophical speculations may be combined with the great revealed doctrines of Christianity in order to form a religion for India?

Undoubtedly the very doubts and uncertainties, the very errors and faltering guesses of Indian philosophy, bear witness to men's need for the truth of the Gospel. But the Gospel must be accepted as the Good Tidings, as God's answer to the questionings of the human heart, and not as merely a mass of human speculations, as a philosophy nobler indeed, but not one whit more authoritative, than those which have, in such bewildering numbers, arisen in Europe and Asia in ancient and modern times. Pantheism, as is well known, underlies almost all Indian philosophy, just as Dualism does old Persian religious speculations. And, as Robertson of Brighton has well pointed out, the way to refute error is to show the misunderstood truth upon which it is based. In the case of Pantheism this misunderstood truth is the Omnipresence of God. The grand scriptural doctrine that man was created in God's image, that through union with the Incarnate Son of God that image may be restored, and that we by regeneration may become sons of God, may be said to be the answer at once to the Hindū yearnings for *yôga* or union with God (the *Paramâtman* or Highest Spirit), and to the Platonic view that the primal music in man's nature, though now sadly out of tune, may in some way be recovered and restored.[1] Belief in the Transmigration of souls testifies to men's consciousness that the human spirit is immortal, and that death does not end all. The doctrine of *avatâras*, so clearly taught in the Bhagavadgîtâ, for example, is at once confirmed and refuted by the Incarnation of our Lord. Christianity has points of contact with all that is best and truest in all religions and in all philosophies, just because it is God's authoritative answer to the yearnings and the questionings of human hearts and minds. We therefore most fully

[1] Πᾶς γὰρ ὁ βίος τοῦ ἀνθρώπου εὐρυθμίας τε καὶ εὐαρμοστίας δεῖται (*Protag.* 326 B).

agree with Professor Max Müller in holding that "What India wants is the young and vigorous Christianity of the first century, not the effete Christianity of the fifteenth century, still less its poor modern imitations."[1] But, for this very reason, feeling that Keshub Chunder Sen was right when he said that "India needs *Christ*," we protest against the theory that any watering down of the historical Christianity of the Gospels can possibly satisfy the needs of Hindū, Buddhist or Muslim. Christianity is not a philosophy, it is the answer to all philosophies, it is *Life*.

It is a remarkable and deeply significant fact that no system of philosophy has ever commanded or can ever command the assent of any large proportion of the human race. Buddhism was in its origin a philosophy,—an Agnostic rather than an Atheistical philosophy,—but ere it could spread to Ceylon, China, or Japan it was obliged to become a religion, with Gautama (Pālī *Gotamo*) Buddha himself as one of its gods. Even in this form it had to coexist, often in the same mind, with Taouism, Shintoism, and perhaps other forms of faith. One reason of this doubtless is that "Divine Philosophy" claims to address itself not to the multitude, but merely to an elect circle of thoughtful minds. But this is not the only reason. The human mind—the instincts of the race—demands a *Religion*, a revelation from One higher than man, something which, instead of giving men mere speculations about the Divine, may bring them into some kind of *connexion* with the God to whose existence their spirits testify, and for whose approval their souls yearn. They need Divine *authority* for their creed: they require something *certain* and not merely probable. Men have in all ages felt that no mortal can possibly teach men to know God and to do His will, unless he has been Divinely illumined and Divinely commissioned. They have felt that the facts of human sorrow and suffering, of human sin and death, are too real to be explained away by any chain of reasoning. This feeling is a wise and true one, for philosophy, however entrancing and however beautiful, is an appeal to the mind and reason, not an answer to the dumb questionings of heart and spirit. Religion alone—all religion in some measure—attempts to do that; hence men have in all ages demanded a religion and accepted its teachings, because they have believed in its Divine origin and authority. In the

[1] *Cosmopolis*, August 1898, p. 335.

very essence of things there is this difference between religion and philosophy, that religion claims to be from God, philosophy openly professes its merely human origin; religion demands our assent under penalty of the Divine disapproval, Philosophy appeals to our reason, and declares that, if we do not admit her claims, we show ourselves to belong to the common herd, the unenlightened multitude, that has no faculties to understand the sublime.

Now, Christianity when subjected to this test is distinctly and indubitably not a philosophy but a religion. Christ did not appeal to a learned inner circle but to the multitude; not to Reason but to Conscience, not to the intellect but to the heart. From one end of the Gospel to the other we find Him asserting in the very clearest terms that He spake with the Father's authority, that He Himself came to reveal the Father, that none could draw near to the Father except through Him, that He and the Father are one. Contrast this with the language of Buddha, for example, as contained in the Mahâparinibbâna-sutta, and the difference will be at once evident. Christ's claim may be accepted or denied, but it can never be explained away. No one who accepts the Gospels merely as he accepts the *Memorabilia* of Xenophon can avoid the conclusion that, whereas Socrates, however erroneous certain of his teachings may have been, was undoubtedly one of the wisest and best of men, Christ, if His teachings are incorrect, must take rank in a very different category. His claims are either true or false. With regard to them we are given no choice. We must as reasonable men come to one of two conclusions; we must either assert with the Jews that "He deceiveth the people," or we must fall at the feet of the Crucified, and with Thomas exclaim, "My Lord and my God."

It is on this account that every attempt to form an eclectic system with a philosophical Christianity as one of its constituents must ever fail, as it has ever failed. Justin Martyr, we are told, continued to wear his philosopher's cloak long after he had embraced the Gospel, because, as he himself informs us, he found in it the only true philosophy.[1] But he did not endeavour to amalgamate the Christian faith with Platonism, to place Christ on a level with Plato. Nay rather, he held that philosophy was his παιδαγωγός to lead him to Christ; he

[1] Ταύτην μόνην εὕρισκον φιλοσοφίαν ἀσφαλῆ τε καὶ σύμφορον., *Dial. cum Tryphone*, cap. viii.

grasped the Divine hand that raised him from the billows and landed him on the rock of Truth; and he was glad, when the time came, not to patronise Christ, but to lay down his life for Him. In the same way many of us have acknowledged the charm of philosophy, and have hung on the utterances of Socrates, of Plato, of Marcus Aurelius, finding much to learn from them all, much to thank God for in their teachings. So may many a Hindū, a Buddhist, a Confucian, a Ṣûfî, cling lovingly to all that is true and noble in the doctrines of the Vedânta, of the Dhammapada, of the Lun Yu, of the Maṣnavî, and—as a Persian poet says—love all the better the scent of the rose because its sweetness tells of the nightingale. But no philosophy can take the place of Him Who is Himself the Way, the Truth, and the Life, for no philosophy can lead us to God—except, indeed, by making us feel our need of Jesus Christ, to Whom philosophy and heathenism as well as Judaism bear witness.

History, ancient and modern, speaks with no uncertain voice as to the possibility of forming a substitute for the simple gospel of the historical Christ. What attempt to unite the morality of the Gospel with any form of philosophic Theism has ever succeeded in the world? Our libraries are filled with the records of the failure of such systems. Manichaeism in the East and Neo-Platonism in the West are among the best known of these futile efforts in the past. Our own age has seen in India the rise, and already sees the waning, of the Brâhmo-Samâj, the Prârthana Samâj, the Ârya Samâj, and other similar attempts to modify Christianity and to adapt it to the needs—the supposed and not the real needs—of the Hindū, who is too proud to enter the Kingdom of Heaven as a little child, as a Paul of Tarsus, an Augustine, a Clement of Alexandria did. Young Japan is busily engaged in something similar. Vast numbers among ourselves are striving, each for himself, to find or invent some *via media* between accepting and rejecting Jesus of Nazareth. His teaching they will accept, if they may omit His Divine claims, His miracles, His atoning death, His resurrection, His promised return to judge the world. A Christianity adapted to the spirit of the age, to the wisdom of the twentieth century, a religion without dogma, and that calls for no exercise of faith, no confession of sin, no denial of self, no taking up of the Cross, is loudly demanded not in India alone, but in Europe as well. Men forget how often the experiment has been tried and has failed. They fail to see that a religion which ignores or denies the most painful and ignominious facts of our fallen nature can never satisfy and can never heal. The lost harmony between the soul and its Creator can never be restored by ignoring the discord. The narrowness of Christianity was denounced by Romans and Greeks alike in the past, just as it is now denounced by so many, both in England and in India. The preaching of the Cross of Christ was to the Jews a stumbling-block and to the Greeks foolishness, and it is so still to their successors. Yet an increasing number in India, in China, in Japan to-day know by their own experience that Christ is "the power of God, and the wisdom of God: because the foolishness of God is wiser than men, and the weakness of God is stronger than men."[1] Hence it is that, amid the wrecks of all human philosophies and theosophies, His promise is fulfilled Who spake as never man spake, "Heaven and earth shall pass away, but My words shall not pass away."[2]

It is surely time to give up the fruitless attempt to construct a new religion, and to learn from our many failures the lesson they should teach. Our human φιλοσοφία, if worthy of the name, should lead us to accept the Divine Σοφία. No philosophical τὸ θεῖον—no *brahman*, to use the Hindū term—can ever take the place of our Father in heaven. No collection of beautiful sayings, of exquisite philosophic guesses at truth, can comfort one mourner, can regenerate one sinner, can give peace to the remorseful and repentant, can give life to our souls, can illuminate the darkness of the tomb. *These things have been tried and have failed.* The human race has grown old in the fruitless attempt to satisfy its hunger with a stone. Philosophies rise one after another, they do their work for good or ill, but they all fade and pass away. Only the Gospel lives on, as fresh, as vigorous, as life-giving to-day as when in ages gone by it gave life and health to the nations which overthrew the effete empire of Rome. And why? Because "it is not a theory, a splendid guess, but a proclamation of facts."[3] And for this very reason it cannot be brought into union with human theories and amalgamated with human philosophies. In a manner, of course, it is true that the Christianity of a nation takes to some extent its colouring from the idiosyncrasy, the habits, the mental characteristics of

[1] 1 Cor. i. 23–25. [2] St. Luke xxi. 33.
[3] *Religious Thought in the West*, Westcott, p. 345.

the people. The religion of Scotland differs in some degree from that of England, the faith of an Augustine from that of an Origen. Christianity to St. Paul presented itself in an aspect not in every respect the same as that under which it appeared to St. John. "All things to all men" is, when properly understood, a law of the faith of Christ, for Christianity is a *life*, not a system of morals, of doctrines, of rites and ceremonies. Yet when the attempt to "adapt" Christianity to men's wishes and fancies rather than to apply it to the needs of their souls is wrongly made, when in a word the Gospel is perverted by the attempt to incorporate into it foreign elements, the result is not good. The present state of the Greek and Roman Churches, resulting in a measure from the conscious or unconscious admission of heathen elements, shows clearly enough the truth of the old saying, *Corruptio optimi pessima.* The teaching of Christ, like the light to which He compared Himself, does not admit of admixture with anything else. Like the light of the sun, too, it is composed of various rays, it may be resolved by the spiritual prism into parts of varying splendour adapted to different minds, and perhaps in a measure to different ages of the world. It may assume a different aspect in consequence of the medium through which it shines. Yet its essence must remain unaltered, or the result is but another of the more than Protean varieties of falsehood with which unhappy mankind have so long deceived themselves. We may, if we will, cull flowers from the Gospel and entwine them gracefully and prettily with those of human philosophies and religious systems —as has been done both in Europe and in Asia—but the result is only a charming bouquet which soon loses scent and freshness. The nations of this sorrowful and sin-stained earth need not this for their healing, for there is no healing in it. Nought can heal but the leaves of the Tree of Life which is in the midst of the Paradise of God.

In conclusion, let us hear the words of one of the learned thinkers of our own day and generation, who cannot certainly be accused of any undue partiality for the Gospel. "The conscience of our day," says James Darmesteter, speaking of the state of things in France, "in uprooting Christianity has uprooted itself. Hence the wail which fills our age, the wail of the orphan who has no longer a Heavenly Father to speak to him and to guide him. It sounds forth from one end of the century to the other, amid the din of wars and of revolutions, amid the triumphant shoutings of science, amid the sarcasms of egoism and of scepticism, amid the ceaseless clamour of life which runs its course. . . . Lo! the century (*i.e.* the nineteenth) at its waning begins to murmur words of faith, goes in search of a revelation, from Ibsen to Tolstoi, from Buddha-Gayā to Fiesole, greets with lofty cries a formless deity who comes not, and strives to join its hands together to repeat a creed which it no longer believes. . . . To-day also do the fair virgins and young men (Amos viii. 12, 13) look in vain from one sea to another; from no rock gushes forth the spring at which to quench the thirst of the soul. The Divine word is not in Ibsen, nor is it even in Tolstoi, and neither from the north nor from the east comes their light."[1]

Whither then shall we turn amid the darkness but to Him who has said, in words which still echo through the ages, "I am come a Light into the world, that whosoever believeth on Me should not abide in darkness,"[2] and who in Himself offers to the thirsty the draught of the water of life freely?

[1] *Les Prophètes d'Israël*, Preface, pp. iii and iv.
[2] St. John xii. 46.

APPENDICES

APPENDIX I

LANGUAGES OF INDIA (INCLUDING FURTHER INDIA).

THE languages of India are so very numerous that we must content ourselves with a brief account of their main family divisions. For a fuller account the student is referred to Dr. Cust's essay on "The Languages of the East Indies," contained in his *Linguistic and Oriental Essays.*

I. The languages of the *Ȃryan* family in India are subdivided into three classes: (1) Pre-Sanskṛitic, (2) Īrānic, (3) Indic. The first of these includes the dialects of the Siyāh-pūsh Kāfirs and of the Dards. Under the Īrānic (so termed as being more closely related to the older Persian than to Sanskṛit) are included the Pašhto or Afghān and the Bilōchī. The chief ancient language of the Indic group is the Sanskṛit. From this various Prākṛit or vulgar dialects sprang: the chief of these was the ancient Magadhī, which was the parent of the Pālī and of the modern Marāṭhī and Sinhalese. From other Prākṛits are descended Kashmīrī, Sindhī, Brahūī, Panjābī, Gujarātī, Uriya, Hindūī, Urdū, Bengālī, and Assamese. There are two main dialects of Kashmīrī, the Pahāṛī, and the Kishtwārī. Hindūī has ceased to be spoken, but is represented by Hindī, with its dialects of Nipālī and Marwārī.

II. To the *Drāviḍian* family belong the Tamil, Telugu, Kanarese, Malayālim, Tulu, Gōnd, K'hond, Orāon, and Rājmahalī languages, with their dialects.

III. The *Kōlarian* family includes the Santāl, Mundārī or Kōl, Juang, Korwa, Kur, Savāra, Mehto, Gadaba, and Mālpahāria languages and dialects.

IV. The *Tibeto-Barman* family contains some 80 languages, divided into the following eight geographical groups:—

1. The Nipāl group includes 13 languages.
2. The Lepcha or Rong . 1 language.
3. The Assam . . . 16 languages.
4. The Manipur-Chittagong 24 „
5. The Barma (Burmese) . 9 „
6. The Tibetan . . 8 „
7. The Chinese . . 7 „
8. The Island . . . 10 „ (Andamanese etc.).

V. The K'hāsī family contains 1 language and 4 dialects.

VI. The Tai or Shān family contains 7 languages (Siamese etc.).

VII. The Mon-Anam family includes 20 languages (Peguan etc.).

VIII. The Malāyan family is divided into 10 groups, the Malay being the main language.

APPENDIX II

A SELECT BIBLIOGRAPHY OF INDIA.

NOTES.—(1) Books which deal with more subjects than one are often mentioned under each head. (2) The student should study the Sacred Books of the various religions in their original languages, and not merely in the translations given in this list.

1. *Early Authorities on India.*

Megasthenes, "Indica."
Arrian, "Voyage of Nearchus."
—— "Indica."
"Periplus Maris Erythraei."
Ctesias, "Indica."
Strabo, Book xv.
Ptolemy, "Geographia" (sections referring to India).
Plutarch (for Alexander the Great's Letters).
Clement of Alexandria.

Origen.
Jerome.
Eusebius.
Philostorgius.
Cosmas Indicopleustes.
Friar Odoric of Pordenone (A.D. 1316–1330).
John of Monte Corvino (1247–1327).
Friar Jordanus (left Europe 1330), "Mirabilia Descripta" ("Wonders of the East," translated by Sir Henry Yule).
Marco Polo (Travels of: ed. by Col. Sir H. Yule, 2 vols. London: John Murray, 1875).
John Marignolli (*circa* 1290–1355).
Ibn Batuta (1304–1378).
Sir John Mandeville (1322–1356).
Nicolo Conti (1419–1440).
'Abdu'r Razzâq (about the same period).
Nikitin (1468–1474).
Hieronomo di Santo Stefano (1494–1499).
Ludovico Varthema (1503–1508).
"Voyages of Joseph the Indian" (Venice).
Pietro Delavalle's Travels (see Terry's account of English conduct in India, prefixed to Eng. trans.).

2. *History of India*

Allen, D. O., "India, Ancient and Modern." Boston, U.S.A., 1858. $2.00.
Andrew, W. P., "India and Her Neighbours." London: Allen & Co., 1877. 15s.
Beveridge, H., "History of India." London, 1862. 3 vols. £3, 3s.
Carlos, E. S., "Short History of British India." Cambridge Warehouse, 1890. 7s. 6d.
Christlieb, T., "The Indo-British Opium Trade and its Effects." London: Nisbet, 1881. 2s.
Cox, Sir G. W., "History of the Establishment of British Rule in India." London: Longmans, 1881. 2s.
Cunningham, H. S., "British India and its Rulers." London: Allen, 1881. 2s.
Dowson, John, "Classical Dict. of Hindū Mythology." London: Trübner. 16s.
Duff, Dr., "The Indian Rebellion." 2nd ed. 1858.

Dutt, R. C., "A History of Civilisation in Ancient India." London: Trübner, 1889–90. 3 vols. £1, 4s.

Eden, C. H., "India, Historical and Descriptive." London: Ward, 1876. 3s. 6d.

Elliot, H. M., "History of India told by its own Historians." London: Trübner, 1867–77. 8 vols. £1, 4s. each. Sequel by E. C. Bayley. London, 1886.

Elphinstone, M., "History of India." London, 1811. 2 vols. 5th edition by Cowell. Murray, 1866. 1 vol. 18s.

—— "The Rise of the British Power in the East." Ed. by Colebrooke. London: Murray, 1887. 16s.

"Encyclopaedia Britannica." Vol. xii., art. "India" (Sir W. W. Hunter).

Fenge, F. R. (Mrs.), "History of India." Boston, U.S.A.: Lothrop, 1881. $1.50.

Grant, Jas., "Cassells' Illustrated History of India." London: Cassells. 2 vols. 1887. 18s.

Haug, M., "Essays on the Language and Religion of Pārsīs." 3rd ed. London: Trübner. 16s.

"Historical Sketch of the Princes of India." London: Smith & Elder, 1833. 7s.

Hodgson, B. H., "Aborigines of India." London: Williams & Norgate, 1860. 9s.

—— "Miscellaneous Essays." London: Trübner. 2 vols. £1, 8s.

Hunter, Sir W. W., "The Annals of Rural Bengal." London: Trübner, 1868–73. 3 vols. £2, 7s.

—— "England's Work in India." London: Smith & Elder, 1881. 1s.

—— "The Indian Empire." London: Trübner, 1886. £1, 1s.

—— "A Brief History of the Indian Peoples." London: Frowde, 1882. 3s. 6d.

James, W. M., "The British in India." London: Macmillan, 1882. 12s. 6d.

Karaka, D. Framjī, "Hist. of the Pārsīs." London: Macmillan, 1884. 2 vols. £1, 16s.

Kaye and Malleson, "History of the Indian Mutiny." London: Allen, 1888-90. 6 vols. £1, 16s.

Kaye, Sir John, "History of the Sepoy War in India." 2 vols.

Keene, H. G., "The Fall of the Moghul Empire." London: Allen, 1876. 10s. 6d.

—— "The Turks in India." London: Allen, 1879. 12s. 6d.

Lacroix de Marlès, J., "Histoire Générale de l'Inde Ancienne et Moderne." Paris, 1828. 8 vols.

Lefmann, S., "Geschichte des alten Indiens." Berlin, 1890. 20 Marks.

Lethbridge, Sir R., "A Short Manual of the History of India." London: Macmillan, 1881. 5s.

Macdonell, A. A., "A History of Sanskṛit Literature." London: Heinemann, 1900. 6s.

Macfarlane, C., "History of British India." London: Routledge, 1881. 3s. 6d.

Maffeus, J., Historiarum Indicarum Libri." Cologne, 1593.

Malcolm, J., "Political History of India." London: Murray, 1882. 2 vols. £1, 12s.

Malleson, G. B., "History of the French in India." London: Longmans, 1868. 16s.

—— "Essays and Lectures on Indian Historical Subjects." London: Trübner, 1876. 5s.

—— "The Indian Mutiny." London: Seeley, 1890.

—— "The Decisive Battles of India." London: Allen, 1888. 7s. 6d.

—— "The Founders of the Indian Empire." Allen, 1882. £1.

—— "The Rulers of India." Macmillan, 1890. 2 vols.

Manning, Mrs., "Ancient and Mediaeval India." London: Allen, 1869. 2 vols. £1, 10s.

Marshman, J. C., "Hist. of India." London: Blackwood, 1867. 3 vols. £1, 2s. 6d.

—— "Abridgement of the History of India." Edinburgh: Blackwood, 1880. 6s. 6d.

Martineau, H., "Sketch of British Rule in India." London: Smith & Elder, 1869. 1s.

Mill, Jas., "History of British India." London, 1858. 5 vols. £2, 14s.

Murray, H. (and others), "Historical and Descriptive Account of British India." London: Nelson, 1854. 6s. 6d.

Noer, F. A., "Kaisar Akbar." Leiden, 1881–90. 2 vols. 20 Marks.

Norwood, S., "Our Indian Empire." London: Tinsley, 1877. 7s. 6d.

Pearce, W. C., "History of India," for Schools. London: Collins, 1876. 1s. 6d.

Pope, G. U., "Text-Book of Indian History." London: Allen, 1880. 12s.

Rousselet, L., "India and its Native Princes." London: Bickers, 1881. 15s.
Sachot, O., "La France et l'Empire des Indes." Paris, 1877. 2 Francs.
Savile, B. W., "How India was Won." London: Hodder, 1881. 5s.
Seeley, "The Expansion of England." London; Macmillan. 5s.
Taylor, Col. M., "History of India." London: Longmans, 1877. 7s. 6d.
Trotter, L. J., "History of India." London: S.P.C.K., 1890. 6s.
—— "History of India under Queen Victoria." London: Allen, 1887. 2 vols. £1, 10s.
Weber, A., "History of Indian Literature." 3rd ed. London: Trübner. 10s. 6d.
Wheeler, J. T., "History of India." London: Trübner, 1867–1881. 4 vols. £4, 3s.
—— "Rise of British Empire in India." Trübner: 1878. 15s.
—— "Short History of India." Macmillan, 1880. 12s.
—— "India under British Rule." Macmillan, 1886. 12s. 6d.
—— "Indian History." Macmillan, 1890.
Williams, Sir M. Monier-, "Modern India and the Indians." London: Trübner. 14s.

3. *Manners and Customs, Missions, Biography*

Allen and M'Clure, "Two Hundred Years." London: S.P.C.K., 1899. 10s. 6d.
American Evangelical Mission in India: Historical Sketch of. Madras, 1879.
Anderson, R., "Missions of A.B.C.F.M. in India." Boston, U.S.A., 1874. $1.50.
Baierlein, E. R., "Die evangelisch-lutherische Mission in Ostindien." Leipzig, 1874. 4 Marks. (Eng. translation by J. D. B. Gribble, "The Land of the Tamulians and its Missions." Madras, 1876.)
Bailey, W. C., "Glimpse at the Indian Mission-Field." London: Shaw, 1886–87. 2s. 6d.
—— "The Lepers of our Indian Empire." Shaw, 1891.
Baptist Missionary Society's Centenary Volume, 1792–1892. Furnival St., London, E.C., 1892.

Barnes, Irene H., "Behind the Purdah." London: Marshall, 1897. 3s. 6d.

Bartlett, S. C., "Missions of the American Board C. For. Missions in India and Ceylon." Boston, U.S.A., 1886.

Bartoli and Maffei, "Life of St. Francis Xavier," tr. by Faber. London, 1858.

Blanchard, S. L., "Yesterday and To-day in India." London: Allen, 1870. 6s.

Bliss, E. M., "The Encyclopaedia of Missions," New York: Funk & Wagnals, 1891. £2, 8s.

Bose, Rām Chandra, "Hindoos as They Are." London: Stanford, 1881. 7s. 6d.

Bradbury, J., "India: its Condition, Religion and Missions." London: Snow, 1884. 4s. 6d.

Bradhead, A., "Historical Sketches of Missions in India" (Presbyterian). Philadelphia, 1881.

Briggs, L., "Sketch of the Pārsīs." London: Simpkin, 1852. 4s.

Brittan, H. G., "A Woman's Talks about India." Philadelphia, 1880. $0.90.

Buchanan, Claudius, "Christian Researches in Asia." London: Cadell & Davies, Strand, 1812.

Buckland, C. T., "Sketches of Social Life in India." London: Allen, 1884. 5s.

Butterworth, H., "Zigzag Journeys in India:" Zenana Tales. Boston, U.S.A.: Estes, 1887. $2.25.

Caird, J., "India: The Land and the People." London and New York: Cassells, 1883. 7s. 6d.

Chambers, Jas., "Bishop Heber and Indian Missions." London: Parker, 1846. 2s. 6d.

Chaplain, Mrs. A. C., "Our Gold Mine": Story of American Baptist Mission in India. Boston, U.S.A., 1879. $1.25.

"Child-Life in India." New York: Sheldon. $0.50.

"Children of India." New York: Revell, 1891. $1.40.

Clark, E. W., "From Hong-Kong to the Himalayas." New York: American Tract Soc., 1880. $1.50.

Clark, R., "Panjāb and Sindh Missions of the C.M.S." Lahore.

Clough, J., "From Darkness to Light." Philadelphia: Amer. Bapt. Publ. Soc., 1882. $1.25.

Clutterbuck, G. W., "In India." London: Ideal Publ. Union, 1897.

Coleridge, H. J., "Life and Letters of St. Francis Xavier." London: Burns & Oates. 2 vols., 1876.
Collins, "Missionary Enterprise in the East." 1873.
Couron, "The Aborigines and Outcasts of India." Calcutta, 1883.
Crellius, H. C., "Oratio: Missae ad Indos Sacrae Legationis Origines et Progressus." Leipzig, 1726.
Cust, Dr. R. N., "A Sketch of the Modern Languages of the East Indies." London: Trübner, 1880. 12s.
Das, Devendra N., "Sketches of Hindoo Life." London: Chapman, 1887. 5s.
Day, L. B., "Govinda Samanta, or Hist. of a Bengal Raiyat." London: Macmillan, 1876. 6s.
—— "Bengal Peasant Life." London: Macmillan, 1878. 6s.
—— "Folk Tales of Bengal." Macmillan, 1883. 4s. 6d.; $1.00.
Douglas, H. A., "Missions in India." London: Gardner, 1877. 2s. 6d.
Duff, Dr. Alex., "India and Indian Missions." Edinburgh: Groombridge, 1839. 12s.
Dubois, "Hindū Manners, Customs and Ceremonies." London: Frowde, 1897. 2 vols. £1, 1s.
—— "Letters on the Indian Rebellion." London: Nisbet, 1858. 3s. 6d.
"Educational Missions in India." Report to Gen. Assembly of Church of Scotland, May 1890.
Ellis, Harriet W., "Our Eastern Sisters." London: R.T.S., 1883. 2s. 6d.
"Entwickelung der Christlichen Missionen in Ostindien." Basel, 1845.
"Etwas vom Indischen Heidenleben." Basel, 1890. 4 Pf.
Fabricii "Lux Evangelii." *Circa* 1700.
Fenger, J. F., "History of the Tranquebar Mission." Tranquebar, 1863.
Framjee Dosabjee, "Hist., Manners, and Religion of the Parsees." London: Smith & Elder, 1858. 10s.
Frere, Sir Bartle, "Indian Missions." London, 1873. 5s.
Gangooly, J. Chunder, "Life and Religion of the Hindoos." Boston, U.S.A., 1861. $1.25.
Gerhard, P., "Geschichte der Mission unter den Kohls." Berlin, 1883. 1–50 Marks.
Germann, W., "Trankebarschen Missionen." Erlangen, 1870.

Germann, W., "Die Kirche der Thomaschristen." Gütersloh, 1877. 15 Marks.

"Geschichte, Neuere, der Ev. Missions-anstalten zur Bekehrung, der Heiden in Ostindien." Halle, 1770–1848. 8 vols. 32 Th.

Glardon, A., "Missions dans l'Inde." Geneva, 1864. 2 Francs.

Gogerly, G., "Pioneer Work in Bengal." London: Snow, 1871. 6s.

Gordon, A., "Our Missions in India" (U.P.). Philadelphia, 1880.

Gracey, J. T., "India: the Country, People, Missions." Rochester, New York, 1884.

Greenfield, M. Rose, "Five Years in Lūdhiāna." London: Partridge, 1886. 2s. 6d.

Handmann, R., "Ev.-Lutherische Mission in Ostindien." Leipzig, 1888. 40 Pf.

Hewlett, Miss S. S., "Daughters of the King." London: Nisbet, 1886. 5s.

"Histoire de l'Etablissement du Christianisme dans les Indes Orientales." Paris, 1803.

Hough, Jas., "Hist. of Christianity in India." London, 1849–60. 5 vols. £2, 18s. 6d.

Hunter, R., "History of Missions of Free Church of Scotland in India and Africa." London: Nelson, 1873. 3s. 6d.

"Indian Female Evangelist." London, Nisbet, 1888–9, etc. etc.

Indian Mission of the Free Church of Scotland, Deputies' Report, 1888, etc.

Jackson, S. M., "Bibliography of Foreign Missions." New York: Funk & Wagnals, 1891.[1]

"Jamunabai's Wanderungen: Blicke in indischen Witwenleben." Basel, 1880. 50 Pf.

Johnston, W., "City, Rice-Swamp and Hill." London Miss. Soc., 1893.

Kaye, Sir John, "Christianity in India."

La Croze, "Histoire du Christianisme des Indes." La Haye, 1758. 2 vols.

Lawrence, Lord, "Our Indian Missions." London, 1873.

Leupolt, C. B., "Recollections of an Indian Missionary." London: S.P.C.K., 1873. 1s. 6d.

—— "Further Recollections of an Ind. Missionary." London: S.P.C.K., 1884. 5s.

[1] To this work much of the present Bibliography of India is due.

Lloyd, Helen, "Hindū Women." London, 1881. 2s. 6d.
Lögstrup, "Nyere Danske Mission blandt Tamulerne." Copenhagen, 1885.
—— "Ihle og Siloam." Copenhagen, 1887.
Lowe, Clara M. S., "Punrooty." London: Morgan, 1880. 2s. 6d.
Lyall, Sir A. C., "Asiatic Studies, Religious and Social." 2nd ed., 1884.
MacDonald, "Work of the Free Church among Women of Bengal." Paisley, 1883.
Mackay, Rev. W. S., "Jesuits' Mission in India." (Calcutta Review).
Murdoch, John, "India's Needs." Madras, 1886.
Oman, J. Campbell, "Indian Life." Philadelphia: Gebbie, 1889. $1.75.
Pitman, E. R. (Mrs)., "Indian Zenana Missions." London: Snow, 1880. 6d.
Protestant Missions in India, Burma and Ceylon: Statistical Tables, 1890. Calcutta, 1892.
Rae, Geo. Milne, "The Syrian Church in India." London: Blackwood, 1893.
Rautenberg, "Rundschau über die Geschichte der . . . Mission unter der Tamulen." Leipzig, 1888. 2 Marks.
Report of the Third Decennial Missionary Conference, 1892–1893.
Rice, H., "Native Life in South India." London: R.T.S., 1889. 2s. 6d.
Rowney, H. B., "The Wild Tribes of India." London: De La Rue, 1882. 5s. 6d.
Sherring, M. A., "Hist. of Prot. Missions in India." London.
Sherring, "The Indian Church during the Rebellion." London: Nesbit, 1859.
Smith, Geo., "Life of Wm. Carey." London: John Murray, 1885. 7s. 6d.
—— "The Conversion of India." London: Murray, 1893.
—— "Henry Martyn." London: R.T.S., 1892. 10s. 6d.
—— "Life of John Wilson." London: Murray, 1879.
—— "Life of Alexander Duff." London: Hodder & Stoughton, 1879. 9s.
—— "Stephen Hislop." London, Murray, 1889. 7s. 6d.
S.P.G., Classified Digest of Records, 1781–1892. London: S.P.G. Office, 1893.

Stock, Eugene, "Hist. of the C.M.S." London, 1898. 3 vols. 18s.
Swanston, Captain, "Memoir of the Church of Malayāla" (in Journal of Royal Asiatic Society, 1834–1835).
Venn, Rev. Henry, "Missionary Life and Labours of Francis Xavier." London: Longmans, 1862.
Whitehouse, "Syrian Church of Malabar." 1873.
Williams, Sir M. Monier-, "Modern India and the Indians." Trübner, London: 1879. 7s. 6d.
Wylie, Macleod, "The Urgent Claims of India." London: Dalton, 1853.
Yule, Colonel H., "Cathay and the Way Thither." London: Hakluyt Society, 1866. 2 vols.

4. *Hindūism* (*including Jainism and Sikhism*).

Acharya, Madhana, "Review of Hindū Philosophies." London: Trübner. 10s. 6d.
"Alberuni's India:" Religion, philosophy, literature. London: Trübner, 1888. 2 vols. £1, 16s.
Arnold, Sir Edwin, "Indian Song of Songs" (Bhagavadgîtâ). London: Trübner, 1875. 5s.
—— "Indian Poetry." London: Trübner. 7s. 6d.
Ballantyne, Jas. R., "Christianity compared with Hindū Philosophy." London: Madden, 1859. 8s. 6d.
—— "Sânkhya Aphorisms of Kapila." London: Trübner. 16s.
Banerjea, H. K. M., "The Âryan Witness." Calcutta, 1875. 8s.
Barth, "Religions of India." London: Trübner, 1891. 2nd ed. 16s.
Bergaigne, Abel, "La Religion Védique." Paris, 1877–1883, 3 vols.
Bose, Rām Chandra, "Hindū Philosophy popularly Explained." The Orthodox Systems. London: Funk & Wagnall, 1884. 6s.
—— "Brahmoism." London: Hunt, 1884. 6s.
Bourquin, A., "Le Panthéisme dans les Védas." Paris, 1886. 6 Francs.
Buchon, Jean A., "Religions de l'Inde" (Paris: Pelletau & Maury. Vol. i. of "Histoire Universelle des Religions." 1844–1855, 5 vols.)

Bühler, G., "Die Indische Secte der Jaina." Vienna, 1888. 70 Pf.
—— "Sacred Laws of the Âryas" (Sac. Bks. of the East, vols. ii. and xiv.). Oxford: Clarendon Press.
—— "Manu" (Sac. Bks. of the East, vol. xxv.). Oxford: Clarendon Press.
Burder, W., "History of all the Religions of the World." New York: Harding, 1877. $1.25.
Burnell and Hopkins, "Ordinances of Manu." London: Trübner. 12s.
Burrell, D. J., "The Religions of the World." Philadelphia: Presbyt. Bk. Publ., 1888. $1.25.
Caldwell, Robert, "Christianity and Hindūism." London: S.P.C.K., 1879. 3d.
Chantepie de la Saussaye, P. D., "Lehrbuch der Religionsgeschichte." Freiburg: Mohr. 2 vols. 18 Marks.
Church, R. W., "Sacred Poetry of Early Religions." New York: Macmillan, 1874. $0.50.
Clarke, Hyde, "Serpent and Šiva-Worship." London: Trübner, 1882. 1s.
Clarke, J. F., "Ten Great Religions." Boston, U.S.A., 1870–1886. 2 vols. $4.00.
Cox, G. W., "Mythology of Âryan Nations." London: Longmans, 1878. 2 vols. £1 8s.
Cust, R. N., "Life of Bābā Nānak." Bombay, 1874. 6s.
Davies, J., "Hindū Philosophy, the Ṣānkhya-Kārikā." London: Trübner, 1881. 6s.
—— "The Bhagavadgītā." London: Trübner, 1882. 8s. 6d.
Deussen, P., "Das System des Vedānta." Leipzig, 1888. 12 Marks.
Ellinwood, F., "Oriental Religions and Christianity." London: Nisbet, 1892.
"Essai sur le Jainisme par un Jain." Leiden, 1885. 2 Francs.
"Faiths of the World" (St. Giles Lectures). Edinburgh: Blackwood, 1882. 5s.
Floyer, A. M., "Evolution of Ancient Hindūism." London: Chapman, 1888. 2s. 6d.
Forbes, A., "Religions of India." Edinburgh, 1865. 1s.
Gough, A. E., "Philosophy of Upanishads." London: Trübner. 9s.
Hardwick, Chas., "Christ and other Masters." New York: Macmillan, 1873. $3.00.

Hopkins, "The Religions of India." London, 1895. 10s. 6d.
Jacob, Geo. A., "Manual of Hindū Pantheism" (translation of the Vedāntasāra). London: Trübner, 1878. Boston, U.S.A., 1881. 6s, $2.50.
Jacobi, Horm., "The Gāma-Sūtras" (Sac. Bks of the East, vol. xxii.). Oxford: Clarendon Press.
Johnson, S., "Oriental Religions," India. Boston, U.S.A.: Osgood, 1872. $5.00.
Jolly, Julius, "Institutes of Vishṇu" (Sac. Bks. of the East, vol. vii.). Oxford: Clarendon Press.
—— "Narada," etc. (Sac. Bks. of the East, vol. xxxiii.). Oxford: Clarendon Press.
Kelang, K. T., "The Bhagavadgītā," (Sac. Bks. of the East, vol. viii.). Oxford: Clarendon Press.
Kern, H., "Saddharma-Pundarīka" (Sac. Bks. of the East, vol. xxi.). Oxford: Clarendon Press.
Kuenen, A., "National Religions and Universal Religions" (Hibbert Lectures). London: Williams & Norgate, 1882. 10s. 6d.
Leigh, H. S., "Religions of the World." London: Trübner, 1869. 2s. 6d.
Macdonald, "The Vedic Religion."
Maurice, F. D., "Religions of the World" (Boyle Lectures). London: Macmillan, 1877. 5s.
Mitchell. J. M., "Hindūism Past and Present." London: R.T.S., 1885. 4s.
Muir, John, "Sanskṛit Texts on Origin and History of People of India." London: Trübner. 5 vols. 1873, etc. £1, 1s. each.
Mujandar, C., "Faith and Progress of the Brahmo-Samāj." Calcutta, 1882. Rs. 2.
Mullens, J., "Religious Aspects of Hindū Philosophy." London: Smith & Elder, 1860. 9s.
—— "Vedāntism, Brāhmaṇism and Christianity compared." Calcutta, 1852.
Müller, F. Max, "The Upanishads" (Sac. Bks of the East, vols. i. and xv.). Oxford: Clarendon Press.
—— "Vedic Hymns" (Sac. Bks. of the East, vol. xxxii.).
—— "Lectures on Science of Religion." London: Longmans, 1873. 10s. 6d.
—— "Origin and Growth of Religion." London: Longmans, 1879. 10s. 6d.

Müller, F. Max, "Natural Religions." London: Longmans, 1889. 10s. 6d.
Non-Christian Religious Systems. London: S.P.C.K. 1876–1899, "Hindūism." 2s. 6d.
Oldenberg, H., "Grihya-Sūtras" (Sac. Bks. of the East, vols. xxiv. and xxx.). Oxford: Clarendon Press.
Padmanjī, Bābā, "Manual of Hindūism." Bombay, 1883.
Pleisch, A., "Die Religion und Philosophie der Indier." Chur. 1881. 2 Marks.
Rāi Bahādur Lāla Bhaj Nāth, "Hindūism Ancient and Modern." Mīraṭh, 1900. London: Luzac & Co. 2s. 6d.
Reid, J. M., "Doomed Religions." New York: Phillips, 1884. $1.50.
Réville, Alb., "Prolegomena of the Hist. of Religions." London: Williams & Norgate, 1884. 10s. 6d.
Rhode, J. G., "Ueber Religiöse Bildung, Mythologie und Philosophie der Hindūs." Leipzig, 1827. 2 vols.
Robson, J., "Hindūism and its Relation to Christianity." Edinburgh: Hamilton, 1874. 7s. 6d.
"Sacred Books of the East," Eng. translations, edited by Prof. Max Müller, on Hindūism, vols. i., ii., vii., viii., xii., xiv., xv., xxii., xxv., xxvi., xxix., xxx., xxxii., xxxiii., xxxiv., xxxviii., xli., xlii., xliii., xliv., xlv., xlvi., xlviii. Oxford: Clarendon Press.
Schermerhorn, M. K., "Sacred Scriptures of the World." New York: Putnam, 1883. $3.00.
Schmidt, H. C., "The Vedas." New York, 1884.
Sen, Keshub Chunder, "The Brahmo-Samāj." London: Allen & Co., 1870. 2s.
Ṣrimat Vidyaraṇya Svāmī, "Panchadāsī," tr. by Nandalāl Dhole. 2 vols., Calcutta, 1900–1901. 5s. per vol.
Trumpp, E., "Die Religion der Sikhs." Leipzig, 1881. 3 Mks.
—— "Nānak." Münich, 1876.
—— "The Ādi Granth." London: Trübner, 1877. £2, 12s. 6d.
Vaughan, J., "The Trident, the Crescent and the Cross." London: Longmans, 1876. 9s. 6d.
Wilkins, W. J., "Hindū Mythology." London: Thacker, 1882. 10s. 6d.
—— "Modern Hindūism." London: Unwin, 1877. 16s.
Williams, Sir M. Monier-, "Indian Wisdom." Luzac, 4th ed. 2s.
—— "Buddhism, Brāhmaṇism, and Hindūism." London: Murray, 1889. £1, 1s.

—— "Brāhmaṇism and Hindūism." London, Murray, 1887. 10s. 6d.
Wynkoop and Wilson, "Christianity and Hindūism." New York, 1877.

5. *Buddhism.*

Alabaster, "Wheel of the Law." London: Trübner, 1871. 14s.
Alwis, J. D., "Buddhism." London: Williams, 1863. 6s.
—— "Buddhist Nirvāṇa." Colombo, 1871.
Bastian, A., "Der Buddhismus in seiner Psychologie." Berlin, 1882. 7.50 Marks.
Beal, S., "Life of Hiuen Tsiang." London: Trübner. 10s.
—— "Texts from the Buddhist Canon." London: Trübner. 7s. 6d.
—— "Buddhist Records of the Western World." London: Trübner. 2 vols. £1, 4s.
—— "The Romantic History of Buddha." Trübner, 1875.
—— "Fo-Sho-Hing-Tsan-King" (a Life of Buddha from the Chinese-Sanskṛit) (Sac. Bks. of the East, vol. xix.). Oxford: Clarendon Press, 1883. 10s. 6d.
Bigaudet, Bp., "Life and Legend of Gaudama." London: Trübner, 1888. 2 vols. £1, 1s.
—— "The Order of Buddhist Monks." London: Trübner, 1866.
Bühler, G., "The Discovery of Buddha's Birthplace" (Athenaeum for March 6, 1897).
—— "Three New Edicts of Aśoka." Bombay, 1877. 3s.
Bunsen, Baron E. de, "The Angel Messiah of Buddhists, Essenes and Christians." London: Longmans, 1880. 10s. 6d.
Cobbold, A., "Shintoism, Buddhism and Christianity." London: S.P.C.K. 2s. 6d.
Collins, M., "Das Lied von der Weissen Lotus." Leipzig: Grieben, 1890. 1.80 Mark.
Copleston, Bp., "Buddhism Primitive and Present." Longmans, 1892.
Dahlmann, J., "Buddha." Berlin, 1898. 6s.
Dods, Marcus, "Mohammed, Buddha and Christ." London: Hodder, 1886. 2s. 6d.
Edkins, "Chinese Buddhism." London: Trübner. 18s.
Eitel, E., "Buddhism." Hong-Kong, 1873.

Elkund, J. A., "Nirvāṇa." Leipzig, 1899. 6s.
Ellinwood, F., "Oriental Religions and Christianity." London: Nisbet, 1892.
"Faiths of the World" (St. Giles Lectures). Edinburgh: Blackwood, 1882. 5s.
Fausböll, V., "The Sutta Nipāta" (Sac. Bks. of East, vol. x.). Oxford: Clarendon Press. 10s. 6d.
—— "Buddhist Birth Stories." Boston, U.S.A.: Houghton, 1881. $5.00. London: Trübner. 18s.
Feer, L., "Etudes Bouddiques." Paris, 1881.
Fradenburgh, J. N., "Living Religions." New York: Phillips, 1890. $1.50.
Grünwedel, "Mythologie des Buddhismus in Tibet und der Mongolei." Leipzig: Brockhaus, 1900.
Hardwick, Chas., "Christ and other Masters." New York and London: Macmillan, 1873. $3.00.
Hardy, "Eastern Monachism." London: Williams, 1864. 7s. 6d., 12s.
—— "Manual of Buddhism in its Modern Development." London: Williams, 1884. £1, 1s.
—— "Legends and Theories of the Buddhists." London: Williams, 1866. 7s. 6d.
—— "Christianity and Buddhism compared." Colombo, 1874.
Jacobi, H., "Der Ursprung des Buddhismus aus dem Sānkhya-Yoga." Göttingen, 1896. 1s. 6d.
Jacobs, J., "Barlaam and Josaphat." London, 1890.
Johnston, S., "Oriental Religions," I. India. Boston, U.S.A., 1872. $5.00.
Kellogg, "Light of Asia and Light of the World." London: Macmillan, 1885. 7s. 6d.
Kistner, Otto, "Buddha and His Doctrines." London, 1869. 2s.
Koeppen, C. F., "Die Religion des Buddha." Berlin, 1857–59. 5th ed. 10 Sgr.
Kuenen, A., "National Religions and Universal Religions" (Hibbert Lectures). London: Williams, 1882. 10s. 6d.
Lillie, A., "Buddha and Early Buddhism." London, Trübner, 1881. 7s. 6d.
—— "Buddha and Buddhism." Edinburgh, 1900. 3s.
Milloné, L. de, "Le Bouddhisme." Lyons, 1882.
Mills, C. D. B., "The Indian Saint" (Buddha). New York: Miller, 1875. $1.50.

Max Müller, "Dhammapada" (Sac. Bks. of East, vol. x.). Oxford: Clarendon Press. 10s. 6d.
Nève, Félix, "Le Bouddhisme." Paris, 1853.
Oldenberg, "Buddha, s. Leben, s. Lehre, s. Gem."
—— Eng. trans. by Hoey. London: Williams, 1882. 18s.
Phillips, R., "Story of Gautama Buddha and his Creed." London: Longmans, 1872. 6s.
Rockhill, W. W., "Udānavarga." Trübner. 9s.
—— "Life of the Buddha." London: Trübner, 1884. 9s.
Rhys Davids, T. W., "Buddhist Suttas" (Sac. Bks. of East, vol. xi.). Oxford: Clarendon Press.
—— "Vinaya Texts" (Sac. Bks. of East, vols. xiii., xvii., xx.). Oxford: Clarendon Press. 10s. 6d. each.
—— "Indian Buddhism" (Hibbert Lectures). London: Williams. 3rd. ed. 1897. 3s. 6d.
—— "Buddhism" (Non-Christian Religious Systems). London: S.P.C.K. 2s. 6d.
"Sacred Books of the East." Ed. by Max Müller. Buddhism, vols. x., xi., xiii., xvii., xix., xx., xxi., xxxv., xxxvi., xlix. Oxford: Clarendon Press.
St. Hilaire, J. B., "Bouddha et sa Religion." Paris, 1866. 3.50 Francs.
Schoebel, Chas., "Le Bouddha et le Bouddhisme." Paris, 1857.
Schott, W., "Ueber den Buddhismus in Hochasien und in China." Berlin, 1846.
Senart, E., "La Légende du Bouddha." Paris, 1882. 15 Fr.
Seydel, Rudolf, "Das Evangelium von Jesu in Verhältnissen zu Buddha-Sage." Leipzig, 1882.
Simpson, W., "The Buddhist Praying-Wheel." London: Macmillan, 1896. 10s.
Stix, H. S., "Christus oder Buddha." Leipzig, 1901.
Summer, M., "Histoire du Bouddha Sakya-Muni." Paris, 1874. 5 Francs.
Tilbe, H. H., "Pālī Buddhism." Rangoon, 1900. 1s. 6d.
Titcomb, Bp., "Buddhism Past and Present." London. R.T.S., 1883. 3s.
Upham, Ed., "The History and Doctrine of Buddhism." London: Ackerman, 1829. £5, 5s.
Virieux, E., "Le Bouddha, sa Vie et sa Doctrine." Paris, 1884. 4 Francs.
Warren, H. C., "Buddhism in Translations." Harvard Oriental Series, 1896. 5s., $1.20.

Wassiljew, W., "Der Buddhismus." St. Petersburg, 1860. 6 Marks.
Williams, Sir M. Monier-, "Buddhism in its Connection with Brāhmaṇism and Hindūism." London, 1889. 10s.
Wurm, Paul, "Der Buddhismus." Gütersloh, 1880. 80 Pf.

6. *Muḥammadanism*

Aḥmad, Sayyid, "Essays on the Life of Mohammed." London: Trübner, 1890.
'Alī, Mīr Ḥasan, "Observations on the Musalmāns of India." London: Allen, 1832. £1, 1s.
Arnold, J. M., "Ishmael." London: Rivington, 1859. 10s. 6d.
Bosworth Smith, "Mohammed and Mohammedanism." London: Smith & Elder, 1889. 7s. 6d.
Derenbourg, H., "La Science des Religions et l'Islamisme." Paris, 1886. 2.60 Francs.
Deutsch, E. O. M., "Islām" (Literary Remains). London: Murray, 1874. 12s.
Dods, Marcus, "Mohammed, Buddha, and Christ." London: Hodder, 1886. 2s. 6d.
Geiger, A., "Was hat Mohammed aus dem Judenthume aufgenommen?" Bonn, 1833.
—— Eng. version by Lady Young. Madras, 1898.
Haines, C. R., "Islām as a Missionary Religion." London. S.P.C.K., 1889 (Non-Chris. Rel. Systems). 2s.
Hauri, J., "Der Islam in seinem Einfluss." Leiden, 1882. 6 Marks.
Hughes, T. P., "Notes on Muhammedanism." London: Allen, 1878, 6s.
—— "Dictionary of Islam." London: Allen, 1885. £2, 2s.
Hunter, W. W., "Indian Musalmāns." London: Trübner, 1876. 12s.
Koelle, S. W., "Mohammed and Mohammedanism." London: Rivington, 1889. 15s.
Krehl, L., "Das Leben und die Lehre des Mohammed." Leipzig, 1884. 6.50 Marks.
Kremer, A. von, "Geschichte der herrschenden Ideen des Islams." Leipzig, 1868. 1 Th. 15 Sgr.
Lake, J. J., "Islām: Its Origin, Genius, and Mission." London, 1878. 5s.

Lees, J. C., "Mohammadanism" (St. Giles Lectures), 1882. Edinburgh.

Lees, W. N., "Indian Mussulmans." London: Williams, 1872. 2s.

Mahomet, Lives of (*see under* Muḥammad).

Matthews, A. N., "Mishqātu'l Maṣâbîḥ." Calcutta, 1809–10, 2 vols.

Muḥammad, Lives of—

Green, S., "Life of Mahomet." London: Tegg, 1877. 3s. 6d.

Irving, W., "Lives of Mahomet and his Successors." London: Murray, 1850. 2 vols. £1, 1s.

Lamairissé et Dujarrac, "Vie de Mahomet d'après la Tradition." Paris, 1897. Luzac (vol. i., 5 Francs.).

Merrick, "Life and Religion of Mohammed." London: Chapman, 1850. 10s. 6d.

Muir, Sir W., "Life of Mahomet." London: Smith & Elder. 3rd ed. 16s.

—— (abridged), 1877. 14s.

—— "Mahomet and Islām." New York: Nelsons, 1884. $1.75.

Nöldeke, "Das Leben Muhammads." Hanover, 1863. 2 Marks.

Prideaux, H., "Life of Mahomet." London, 1798.

Sprenger, "Das Leben Muhammads." Berlin, 1861–65. 3 vols., 12 Marks.

Summers, J. O., "Life of Mohammed." Nashville, 1875. 50 Cents.

Müller, A., "Der Islam in Morgen- und Abendland." Berlin, 1885.

Muir, Sir W., "The Rise and Decline of Islām." London: R.T.S. 4d.

—— "The Caliphate." Smith & Elder, 3rd ed., 1898. 16s.

—— "Annals of the Early Caliphate." Smith & Elder, 1883.

—— "The Mameluke or Slave Dynasty of Egypt." London: Smith & Elder, 1896.

—— "Mahomet and Islām." R.T.S., 3rd ed., 1895. 2s. 6d.

—— "The Mohammedan Controversy." Edinburgh: T. & T. Clark, 1897. 7s. 6d.

—— "The Coran: Its Composition and Teaching." S.P.C.K. 2s. 6d.

—— "The Sources of Islām" (translation). Edinburgh: T. & T. Clark, 1901. 1s. 6d.

Muir, Sir W., "Sweet Firstfruits" (translation). London: R.T.S. 2s. 6d.
—— "Beacon of Truth" (translation). R.T.S. 2s. 6d.
—— "Apology of Al Kindî" (translation). 2nd ed., 1887.
Nöldeke, Th., "Geschichte des Qorâns." Göttingen, 1860.
Osborn, R. D., "Islâm under the Arabs." London: Longmans, 1876. 12s.
—— "Islâm under the Khalifs of Baghdad." London: Seeley, 1880. 10s. 6d.
Pischon, C. N., "Der Einfluss des Islam." Leipzig, 1881. 3 Marks.
Qur'ân, Translations of—
Lane, E. W. (Selections from). London: Trübner, 1879. 9s.
Palmer (Sac. Bks. of East, vols. vi. and ix.). Oxford: Clarendon Press, 1882. £1, 1s.
Rodwell, J. M. London: Quaritch, 1876. 12s.
Sale, G. (Wherry's edition). London: Trübner, 1882.
Robinson, C. H., "Mohammadanism: Has it any Future?" London: Gardner, 1897. 2s.
Sell, Edw., "The Faith of Islām." London: Trübner, 2nd ed. (Trübner's Oriental Series). London: Trübner, 1897. 12s. 6d.
—— "The Historical Development of the Qur'ân." Madras, Rs.2, 3s. 6d.
—— "The New Islâm." Contemporary Review, Aug. 1893.
—— "Essays on Islâm." London: Simpkin, 1901. 4s. 6d.
Stobart, J. W. H., "Islâm and its Founder." London: S.P.C.K. (Non-Christian Religions), 1877. 2s. 6d.
Tisdall, W. St. Clair, "The Religion of the Crescent." London: S.P.C.K. (Non-Christian Religions), 1895. 4s.
Vambéry, H., "Der Islam im 19ten Jahrhundert." Leipzig, 1875. 6 Marks.
Vaughan, Jas., "Trident, Crescent and Cross." Longmans, 1876. 9s. 6d.
Wellhausen, J., "Skizzen und Vorarbeiten." Berlin, 1889. 4 vols. 32 Marks.
Wherry, "Comprehensive Commentary to Qur'ân." London: Trübner. 4 vols. £2, 8s.
Zwemer, S. M., "Arabia, the Cradle of Islâm." London: Oliphant, 1900. 7s. 6d.

INDEX